Course *of* Action

Course *of* Action

A Journalist's Account from
Inside the American League Against
War and Fascism and the
United Electrical Workers Union (UE)
1933-1978

James Lerner

Edited by Richard Neil Lerner
and Anna Marie Taylor

RNL Publishing
Berkeley, California

For my grandchildren
Thea, Liza, Matthew, and Susanna

Printed in the United State of America.

RNL Publishing
2335 Stuart Street
Berkeley 94705
www.RNLpublishing.com

Cover woodblock print © Lynd Ward, courtesy of Robin Ward Savage and Manda Weedon Ward

Design and layout by Margaret Copeland, Terragrafix, Berkeley, CA
Electronic printer files by Jan Camp, Arc Light Books, arclightbooks.com

Lerner, James, 1911-2003
Course of Action: A Journalist's Account from Inside the American League Against War and Fascism and the United Electrical Workers Union (UE) 1933-1978 / James Lerner / edited by Richard Neil Lerner and Anna Marie Taylor
p. cm.
Includes notes and index.
ISBN: 978-0-9786517-9-4
1. Lerner, James—memoir. 2. Antifascism—United States—History.
3. Great Depression—United States—History. 4. Student antiwar movement 1930s—United States—History. 5. Labor unions—United States—History.

Contents

Preface

Editor's Note: *James Lerner, my father and author of this book, died in 2003, before seeing his unpublished manuscript in print. The narrative grew out of a number of sources, including his letters, journals, and transcribed interviews I recorded with him. We discussed the drafts of the manuscript over several years and I promised to one day bring the book to light. My father left the following introduction.*

— Richard N. Lerner

This account covers my family background, four decades as journalist for the United Electrical, Radio and Machine Workers of America (UE) and the development of this union during the period between 1940 and the 1970s. My decision to include my peace advocacy with the American League against War and Fascism during the 1930s, reflects my lifetime dedication to peace as well as labor. The encouragement of others, and my recognition of the rarity of written history about the League, also motivated me to include that era in this book.

My work with the League often meant being away from home for weeks at a stretch. I was newly married at the time, and much of the material for Part One was fortunately preserved because I often wrote to my wife Gertrude in the form of journals.

I begin with some stories of my family history and early school experiences. From there, I relate events as I lived them within the League and later within UE. The League lasted only seven years, and dissolved with the outbreak of the Second World War. The UE, founded in 1936, continues today to advance the rights and benefits of workers.

The history of UE is well known from its many important victories in obtaining better wages and working conditions for its members. UE is also widely known for its steadfast resistance to attacks against its members and officers and threats to its very existence during the McCarthy period. My hope is that this book, told by an insider who spent over four decades as writer and editor for the union, will honor UE's legacy to the union movement and will contribute to a fuller understanding of the uneven progress of American democracy in the twentieth century.

PART ONE

Early Years

CHAPTER ONE

Heritage and Schooling

I treasured the fountain pen and pencil set my father, Louis Lerner, gave me when I entered high school in 1923. Although it had long lost its utility, it always symbolized my father's influence on my lifetime commitment to social justice and peace. My father received this pen set from fellow workers. As their elected union representative, he saw them through decades of grievances and strikes. When he was more than ninety years old, he still liked to repeat stories of his early times with the union.

My father was the youngest of seven surviving sons in a family of thirteen children. They were among the estimated 10,000 Jews who left Russia after the pogroms of Easter Sunday 1881. During 48 hours in over 160 Russian cities and towns, many Jews were slaughtered and others dispossessed. Severe restrictions were imposed on where they could live. My father's family fled to the Austro-Hungarian province of Galicia and settled in the city of Brody.

To safeguard his children's religious heritage, my grandfather refused to let them attend public school. He expected my father to become a *soifer*, a copier of religious texts. This was an ancient craft, painstakingly done by hand. However, my father never fulfilled this destiny. His older brother, Wolf, sent him a steamship ticket from America. He was eighteen years old in 1890 when he set out for Antwerp, Belgium, to board the ship. Three weeks after his arrival on the Lower East Side of New York City, where he temporarily took up residence with his brother, my father began work at a factory where he learned to sew leather suitcases by hand. The other workers were all Irish or German. Within two months of being in the country, my father found himself on his first labor strike.

Along with several other strikers, he was arrested for fighting with scabs who the union believed had been brought from Chicago to break the strike. Knowing my father as a gentle human being who never even spanked his children, I found it difficult to visualize him hitting anyone, even as a youth. Yet he didn't disclaim the police charge. The agreement that settled the strike raised his pay to $4 for a six-day, 59-hour week. Extra pay for overtime would not be won by working people until four decades later, still time for my father to benefit. He had worked at his trade for over 50 years except for two brief attempts to go into business for himself. He once set up a grocery store specializing in tea, coffee, and morel mushrooms imported from Eastern Europe, and another time he became a partner in a leather goods plant.

While my father's memory of his youth centered on his desire to move forward, my mother's memory of her youth fixated on the poverty she knew in the Austrian-Hungarian village of Bialy Kamen where she grew up. Sadie Rothenberg Lerner remembered vivid details of her early life. Her father, a devout orthodox Jew, served the town's rabbi as a *gobbeh* whose duties included writing down applications of petitioners who sought the rabbi's advice on personal problems. He also helped adjudicate disputes with fellow religionists outside the public justice system. The few pennies he earned for this service were not enough to support a family of seven.

The author's father Louis Lerner on his final day of work after more than 40 years as a leather worker. Photograph by James Lerner.

According to my mother, as long as her grandmother, who owned a prosperous general store, was willing to support them, the family was able to get by. But she finally went to the rabbi to demand that her son support his family. The rabbi responded that her son's dedication to God accounted for her prosperity. Another incident that involved this rabbi had a great impact on my grandfather. He often accompanied the rabbi when he traveled to outlying towns. In one of those towns, a tailor made my father a coat similar to the one he had made for the rabbi. Afterwards, when the rabbi's stepdaughter came to the house and told my grandmother that it wasn't proper for a mere *gobbeh* to wear the same kind of coat as a rabbi, my grandmother gave it back to her. When my grandfather came home and heard what had happened, he appeared to have something like a heart attack. He gave up serving God through the rabbi and began teaching Hebrew to private students.

When my mother was 11-years-old, her parents paid the village tailor $10 to take her on as an apprentice. My mother wanted to learn how to use a sewing machine, but when she got there the owners told her the job was only for childcare. But she would not be denied, and every time the tailor's mother went out, she would stand and watch people using the machines. By the second year, they let her use the machines and even began paying her a small amount. The tailor also took my mother along on his trips into the country where he measured peasants for clothing. For her help, people would give my mother vegetables which she brought home for the family.

After three years with the tailor, my mother received a letter from her mother's sister Rifke, who had emigrated to the United States several years before. She urged Sadie to join her. This was an attractive prospect for a 14-year-old who saw ahead only a lifetime of poverty. Bolstered by a safe-voyage prayer her father gave her to say when she saw the ocean, my mother crossed the Atlantic. She arrived in New York City in March 1907. At her aunt's household, there were several other boarders, including Louis Lerner.

My mother soon got a job basting clothing and began earning $4 a week. She also helped with housework at the boarding house and paid her aunt weekly installments on the $50 she spent for the steamship ticket. After she finished paying for the ticket, she started sending a few dollars a week home to her parents.

Jim Lerner's mother, Sadie Rothenberg, in 1908, age 14, first row, far left, at her first job in America, with other workers at a tailor shop.

Three years after my mother arrived in the United States, the leather worker and the skirt baster married in a private wedding attended by a few friends and relatives. During the year they got married, my father was again out on strike, this time for nine months. The workers lost the strike and my father was blacklisted from the trade. He started a retail shop specializing in imported tea, coffee, and morel mushrooms. Ten months after Louis and Sadie got married, I was born in a tenement house at 330 East Houston Street on the east side of lower Manhattan. The house was later torn down to make way for Franklin Delano Roosevelt Drive along the East River.

When I was three years old, we moved uptown into a five-story East Harlem tenement house on Lexington Avenue between 100th and 101st Streets. There my mother soon gave birth to twins, Morris and Jennie. Two years later we went to the country to escape the brutal summer heat of the crowded tenement buildings. One hundred miles northwest in the

Catskill Mountains town of Ellenville, New York, we stayed at a frame building that provided furnished rooms and a communal kitchen for vacationing working class families. Since workers had no vacations, paid or otherwise, my father did not join us. That was the summer of 1916, when polio, first called infantile paralysis, swept across the country.

Alarmed by reports that the disease had reached surrounding communities in the Catskills, we rushed home. Several days later, I was carried down four flights of tenement house stairs by white-coated hospital aides and placed in an ambulance full of other victims of the disease. I was taken to the Willard Parker Hospital for Contagious Disease and quarantined on an East River island.

Press reports of the epidemic told of scores of children dying every day; of other countries barring travelers from New York City; of many colleges and athletic teams being quarantined; and of the disease spreading into most other states. After an extended series of physical therapy treatments at the New York Hospital for Joint Diseases, I finally recovered full use of my limbs but was left with a permanent hand tremor.

A year after leaving the hospital, I enrolled in an all-boys' elementary school two blocks from where we lived. The area was populated by Italian, Jewish, and Irish immigrants. Relations between the Italians and Jews were cordial, even friendly, as religious differences played little part in attitudes toward each other. This was not true, unfortunately, for relations between the Irish and Jewish boys. The Irish sometimes called us "Christ Killer" or used Halloween as an occasion to hit us with chalk-filled stockings. When I was ten, an Irish boy walked up and down the aisles of the classroom one day pressing a crucifix against the lips of every Jewish boy demanding that he kiss it or else. My mother went to the school the next day and protested the incident to school authorities. Despite these memories of ethnic conflict at school, I recall that it was a kind Irish elementary school teacher who eased my path into education by arranging for me to continue in her class.

During my childhood, my father always spoke admiringly of men and women with names like O'Neill, Flynn, and Haywood who were battling oppression as Socialists or leaders of the Industrial Workers of the World

(IWW). He took me to Socialist Party meetings, lectures, and debates where people discussed such subjects as public ownership of industry, capital punishment, and socialism. These things helped me put my school experiences into perspective. My father especially admired Professor Scott Nearing for his courageous opposition to the First World War and his outspoken espousal of socialism.[1]

My mother introduced me to religious studies through an elderly, bearded man who came several times to our flat when I was eight years old. He gave up on me when I kicked him in the shin in response to his pinching my cheek. My father then persuaded my mother to enroll me in a nearby secular Jewish school. This was part of a chain of schools run by the Workmen's Circle, a socialist Jewish fraternal order. Three afternoons a week I went happily to be taught to read, write, and speak Yiddish in an atmosphere of camaraderie. This learning environment contrasted greatly with the harshness and tension I found at public school.

Among the teachers at the Jewish school were poets, fiction writers and composers, whose songs we performed at concerts for family and friends. Like many Jewish workers who came from Europe early in the century, the school's instructors were not religious. This helped reinforce the ideas children like myself were absorbing in their working class homes. A teacher from that era gave me a postcard with a photograph of Karl Marx. On the back, in Yiddish script, I found a note congratulating me on my advancement to fourth grade.

I also enrolled in a Sunday school run by the Socialist Party on Harlem's Madison Avenue. The children's program included labor songs and stories. When Socialist Party and railroad labor leader Eugene V. Debs[2] was released from prison following his Christmas pardon in 1921 by President Warren G. Harding, our teachers took the Sunday school class to hear Debs speak at Madison Square Garden. Debs had just served part of a ten year sentence for making a speech opposing American participation in the First World War. While in the penitentiary in Atlanta, Debs ran for president of the United States and received close to a million votes.

The substantial socialist movement in New York City was also visible in the election of a socialist, Meyer London, to the U.S. Congress in

1916, and five other socialists to the state assembly. They were all expelled from the legislature in 1920 for supporting their party's opposition to the war. I later heard bald-headed August Claessens, one of the ousted legislators, giving a soap box speech at the corner of Madison Avenue and 106th Street in East Harlem. I also remember that by the time I was eleven years old, I could stand at the long wooden table at Socialist Party headquarters and help pack sandwiches for poll watchers.

A favorite working people's orator at that time was Municipal Court Judge Jacob Panken, known for protecting the housing rights of strikers and tenants. When the tenants in our tenement house conducted a rent strike, Judge Panken would not allow the eviction of those who were withholding their rent. I saw him striding from side to side on the platform of the New Star Casino on 107th Street near Park Avenue, east of the New York Central Railroad tracks. He would sometimes get down on one knee, arms outstretched, with his index finger extended and his long grayish hair hanging down in back below his collar, as he denounced the landlords to enthusiastic applause. After one such experience, I came home, mounted a chair in the kitchen, and launched into my own rendition of the judge's speech.

When I was about ten years old, my parents bought me two sets of books. One was a 25-volume set of Mark Twain's writings. The other was comprised of 27 volumes in Yiddish by Sholom Aleichem. He wrote with sharp wit about Jewish people in the villages and towns of Eastern Europe and their experiences as immigrants to the United States. His stories covered such travails as greedy landlords, exploitative employers, and insensitive government bureaucrats. The first book I remember buying for myself was a used copy of Jack London's novel, *The Sea Wolf.* I avidly read his animal and adventure tales as well as his stories about the lives and struggles of working people. I searched for everything that was available by him at the neighborhood public library on 96th Street near Madison Avenue.

On Sundays, my father would often walk with me and my brother and sister to the Metropolitan Museum of Art or the American Museum of Natural History. During summer afternoons, I sometimes went alone to the Polo Grounds, where both the Yankees and the Giants played before Yankee Stadium was built in 1922. From a bleacher seat, I watched Babe Ruth, Bob Meusel, and Jumpin' Joe Dugan of the Yankees—my team! However, I lost my respect for Babe Ruth one afternoon when, along with some other kids, I waited at the players' exit after a game, anxious to get his autograph. The bloated, red-faced Babe pushed past us as he shoved our scraps of paper aside.

On an early February morning in 1923, I awoke to find two infants lying on our round oak dining table. A doctor tended to my mother, who had just given birth to a second set of twins, another boy and girl. Without a job and recently bankrupted in his second attempt at private business, my father despaired over how to pay rent and support two new children. He decided to persuade a distant relative who owed him money to provide us with a rent-free apartment in a house near Coney Island. We moved there after I completed eighth grade. The foundation of the building had settled so much on one side that almost anything dropped at one end of a room rolled downhill to the opposite wall.

On the street level of the building where we were living, facing a broad parkway leading to the ocean, our relative operated two shops. In one, he sold candy and cigarettes and offered patrons the use of illegal slot machines in the back. In the other shop, he operated a billiard parlor frequented by unsavory characters. Next door to our second-floor apartment, men mixed alcohol and coloring agents to produce bootleg whiskey. This of course violated the *Eighteenth Amendment to the Constitution* and the *Volstead Act*, which banned the manufacture and sale of alcohol. I recall that the smell of bathtub whiskey permeated the air of our apartment.

City police occasionally raided the candy store, and our next door neighbors also got raided from time to time by federal agents. The discovery that our relative was giving the various whiskey makers and slot machine users the key to our bathroom soon drove my parents to forego the housing arrangement. We moved several blocks away to the third floor of a frame house. Its only memorable feature was a wooden drum alongside a rear window with a reel and rope. In case of fire the rope was supposed to be tied around one's waist before stepping out the window. There was one drum and one rope for all seven of us. Fortunately, we never needed it.

When we later moved to Brooklyn, I enrolled at Erasmus Hall High School, where the faculty adviser, true to the tradition of the Dutch settlers of Flatbush who founded the school as a private academy in 1787, persuaded me to study Latin. Two years later, I transferred to the newly built James Madison High School. The one thing that stands out from those years was my membership in the Current Events Club, whose members held debates over newspaper stories.

My father finally found work back at his leather trade and managed to put together a down payment on a stucco house on nearby Harvey Court. It faced a fetid tidal marsh from which swarms of mosquitoes rose every summer evening. On the upper floor my parents created a three-room rental flat. This left three lower rooms, including a kitchen, for our family. Because of our proximity to the beach, former Harlem neighbors and relatives from other parts of the city descended on us during the summer to change into bathing suits, return from the beach to shower, and share our food. Coming as they did generally on Saturdays, they would be invited to spend the night so they could go back to the beach on Sunday morning. Wall-to-wall sleepers sometimes covered our floors.

CHAPTER TWO

Experimental College

After graduating from high school, I found a job at Macy's department store and enrolled in evening classes at the Brooklyn branch of the City College of New York. Macy's regular work week was six days long. If overtime was required, as during stock taking, any remuneration was given as a meal in the employee cafeteria. Although I worked only as a stock clerk, I was required to wear a white shirt attached to a stiffly-starched collar by a brass collar button like all other male employees in the store.

Since Macy's had not yet expanded into a nationwide chain, some of the older employees retained an illusion of being close to the store's owners, and often referred to members of the Straus family by their first names. The company president at that time, Jesse Isidor Straus, had succeeded his father Isidor after he and his wife went down with the Titanic.

One of my duties at Macy's was to carry suits to the alteration department on an upper floor. This provided me with opportunities to chat with the tailors. Most of them did not share the department manager's personal attachment to the Straus family. I remember an Irish tailor who sat cross-legged on a wooden table, interrupting his stitching from time to time to dip into a Copenhagen snuff box for a pinch of tobacco. He set this between his lower lip and brown teeth. He would talk about the affairs of the world and his many work-related grievances.

A slim young Italian immigrant stood out among the tailors. The other workers referred to him as "Calabrese," which I took to mean that he was a native of Calabria. He clearly had no use for Mussolini, the fascist dictator who seized control of Italy five years earlier, and he often expressed his contempt in descriptive cursing. I enjoyed the sarcastic banter between Calabrese and the other Italians, as they shouted above the din of the sewing and steam-pressing machines. Then there was the alteration department foreman, a short, hunched man in his sixties, who hobbled from tailor to tailor distributing the work or examining the finished work over the top of glasses resting at the end of his nose. I felt comfortable in this mixed Irish-Italian-Jewish community.

I had been at Macy's about nine months when a small single column item in the *New York Times* reported that an Experimental College at the University of Wisconsin was completing its first year and was seeking students for a second freshman class. I applied and was accepted, as was my closest high school friend, Sidney Slotznick. We left by bus for Madison in September 1928. Sidney and I shared a room in a dormitory overlooking beautiful Lake Mendota.

The Experimental College was established by Alexander Meiklejohn. He had taught philosophy and held various university administrative positions, including president of Amherst College, before he decided to start the Experimental College in Madison. Meiklejohn was born in Rochdale, England, where the cooperative movement was founded when he was a child. He described how groups of textile workers would meet in his home in England on Saturday mornings to discuss their problems and grievances. Meiklejohn's affinity for free discussions and his association with working people had eventually brought him into conflict with the trustees of Amherst College.

Meiklejohn had modified traditional college courses at Amherst in favor of content that encouraged independent thinking. He urged Amherst students to go to textile mills and factories in nearby towns to teach workers how to read and write and to think about how economics and history determined the way they lived. In collaboration with trade unions, Meiklejohn set up classes for workers at Holyoke and Springfield textile mills near Amherst. He riled supporters of U.S. participation in World War I by insisting that opponents of the war be allowed to express their views on campus. He had also outraged members of the Alumni Council by telling them that at Amherst "you will see students playing football, not football players attending college." He caused even more controversy by bringing in British scholars to lecture on socialism.

The Meiklejohn experiment in Madison required that the entire student body of freshmen and sophomore classes, a maximum of 250 students, live together in the same dormitory. As university regulations did not permit men and women to live together, no women attended the College.

There were many memorable events that took place during my stay at the College. One time a student, David Gordon, made some negative public remarks about the right wing views of idolized aviator Colonel Charles Lindbergh. Gordon, a student who attended the College thanks to a scholarship from Wisconsin writer Zona Gale, had once spent time in a New York reformatory for an "obscene" poem about government that had appeared in a communist paper. Rumors that some university students were planning to raid our dormitory to "get" him inspired several Experimental College students who were football players to publicly announce they were prepared to defend Gordon. This evidently worked, because the threatened raid never materialized. Gordon was later one of three Experimental College alumni who served in the Abraham Lincoln Brigade of American volunteers who fought in the Spanish Civil War.

Closeness between faculty and students, which Meiklejohn fostered as part of College experiment, included having unmarried faculty members live in our dormitory. He also encouraged married members to invite students to their homes for social evenings. I remember a visit to the Meiklejohn home, where his wife read poetry.

The two-year Experimental College course consisted of one year of concentration on fifth-century Athens and a second year on 19th-century America. Given the nature of the college and the absence of formal classes, I expanded my reading by spending many hours in the stacks of the State Historical Society on the Madison campus. I took advantage of the large collection of writings on labor and Marxist theory. Many of these works were from the personal libraries of men associated with pioneer 19th-century European socialists.

In the library, I discovered the poetry of Professor William Ellery Leonard of the university's English department. His poems were often about labor organizers such as Eugene Debs and victims of race hatred, including Leo Frank, a Jew who was lynched by a mob in Atlanta, Georgia, in 1915. I also came upon the writings of American author, Upton Sinclair. I had just heard about his novel entitled *Boston*, based on the Sacco-Vanzetti legal case involving two Massachusetts radicals who were executed in 1926. I wrote Sinclair a letter to tell him how much I valued his work. He responded with a note: "Dear Comrade, I have your kind letter. I send you a paperback copy of *Boston* as a gift."

While I was at the Experimental College, I joined the campus Liberal Club, which invited speakers from various political movements, including socialist and communist, to address its members. At that time, I began writing my first journalism pieces. They were letters to the campus daily newspaper, often challenging positions taken by the editor or other writers.

I took a job as a dishwasher at the cafeteria where Experimental College students ate as part of their live-work experience. When a new dime store opened in Madison, I found work there too. But this wasn't enough to meet expenses. Several weeks before the end of the college year, I found a note in my letterbox advising me that I would no longer be able to stay at the college because I owed $51. I wrote home pleading for financial help, but as a result of the economic depression gripping the country, my father was unemployed and support from the family was impossible.

I set out to hitchhike to New York City. The first night out, I slept shoulder to shoulder with a truck driver in his cab, parked at the side of the road. The next night, I sought out the central police station in Pittsburgh to ask whether I could spend the night there. My boldness faded, however, when a policeman swinging a set of keys told me to follow him toward a block of cells. He opened the door to one that already contained several other young fellows and slammed the door. I fell asleep as soon as I hit the floor. Early the next morning, we were hastily ordered to get out.

I took whatever vehicles would pick me up as I made my way east, and arrived in Gettysburg, Pennsylvania, the next afternoon. After making a hurried visit to the Civil War battlefield, I approached a small frame house where a window sign advertised rooms for tourists. The woman who came to the door accepted my offer of a dollar to spend the night. In this way, I made my way toward home where I would join my mother and unemployed father and four siblings. I brought back with me from Madison the final freshman class assignment, planning to return to Madison in the fall. I hoped I could find a way to earn enough money during the summer to meet my school debt and cover the next year. However, since I now became the principal breadwinner, I was never able to find a way to return to the College.

The Experimental College came to an end in June 1932 after only five years. It had enrolled a total of 327 students. The Great Depression sharply reduced the number of students like myself who could attend institutions of higher education. Criticism among campus and state conservatives about the kind of students the college attracted ("radicals and eastern Jews") further undermined support for the college. Although leaving the College abruptly in 1929 for economic reasons was a great disappointment, my associations and correspondence with Alexander Meiklejohn and my fellow students continued to grow in the years that followed. Reunions of Experimental College students and faculty brought many of us together even four or five decades after the College closed.

From pioneer in challenging the shortcomings of higher education, Alexander Meiklejohn went on to become the nation's outstanding legal defender of the *First Amendment to the Constitution*. In 1951, the FBI sought to question him on the loyalty of one of his former pupils, but he refused based on his belief in the *First Amendment*. Meiklejohn was the first speaker at Senate committee hearings on "Security and Constitutional Rights," held in 1955. He presented what later became a classic examination of the meaning of the *First Amendment*. In 1963, this scholar who had once lost the presidency of Amherst College for being too radical in his educational and political beliefs, was awarded the Medal of Freedom by President John F. Kennedy.

In 1955, I visited Meiklejohn at his home in Berkeley, California. He described how he had gone to the U.S. Supreme Court in Washington to be present at the appeal on behalf of Communist Party leaders who had been convicted of conspiring to advocate the overthrow of the U.S. government. During a recess, Justice Felix Frankfurter, his longtime friend, came down from the bench and spoke with Meiklejohn about how difficult the decision was going to be for the judges. Meiklejohn tried to persuade the judge to argue for a decision in the case that would exonerate the defendants and uphold the basic free speech tenets of the *First Amendment.* Unfortunately, the convictions were all upheld. Some of the accused subsequently spent time in prison, and some went underground.

At the time of Meiklejohn's death in December 1964 at age 92 years of age, students at the nearby Berkeley campus were in the middle of a battle with university authorities over the right of student organizations to exercise their *First Amendment* rights on campus. According to Meiklejohn's wife, Helen, he passed away in his chair in the middle of writing a letter to the university in support of the students and the movement that would later become known as the Free Speech Movement.

CHAPTER THREE

Working During the Depression

After I left the Experimental College, I took a job at 20 East Broadway in New York's Chinatown, working in a custom-tailor shop. Men came from the Wall Street area to select cloth from swatches of woolens. Each part of the suit came from a different shop. Every morning, I made the rounds, collected rolled-up cloth that had been cut to order, and carried it all back to the main shop in a black sack. The $20 a week I was paid would prove to be the most I would earn for a long time and was often the mainstay of our family's income.

The tailor shop was named Kaminer and Wachter after its two owners. Kaminer was a stocky man with thick glasses who dealt with the stores and supervised the tailor shop. When there was an urgent need to complete a job, he did some sewing himself. The other owner was a mild-mannered man with radical sympathies who stood at his pressing table all day pounding the jackets at various stages. He used a sixteen-pound "goose" that consumed gas through a rubber tube. His was the kind of work that made hernias an occupational hazard. His views of society's problems were similar to mine, and we would often discuss events of the day while I waited in the shop for my next run to Wall Street.

On the fourth floor of the main shop, a dozen or so highly skilled men, mostly Jewish and Italian, sat cross-legged near long wooden tables doing basting by hand. When I returned the basted jackets to a store, the fitter would take them apart to make adjustments. Finally, several Italian women added button holes by hand while they talked among themselves. When a tiny black-haired woman who was in charge of apportioning the work among the women was unable to come in, I would carry the work several flights up to her tenement apartment a block away. One way or another, I eventually laid completed suits across my arm, covered them with a sheet of brown wrapping paper, and delivered them to the stores that served Wall Street clients.

The world of the tailor shop was strikingly different from the one I came up against when I finally delivered the completed suits. Sometimes I wondered whether the men who ordered several costly suits at a time ever thought about the men and women who produced their clothing or about how the tailor shop was surrounded by slums and tenements where most of the workers lived.

When they came to the stores for fittings, customers often talked of the "market" and offered predictions about when it would rebound from the economic depression. Within the shops, workers talked about rents, landlords, clothing for their children, and the growing fear of unemployment. Workers would surge around me whenever I arrived with the black sack. How much they would earn would directly depend on how much cloth fell out of that sack.

Except for the few times I happened to see a customer impatiently waiting for a rush delivery, I only recall finding out once about the actual personal destination of a suit. This was when I delivered a batch of uniform jackets with brass buttons to banker J. P. Morgan's yacht, aptly named the *Corsair*.

Incidental to my job at the tailor shop was the assignment to purchase a box of chocolates every Friday for a boy named Barry, the twelve-year-old son of Kaminer. About four decades later, I recognized him when Barry Commoner, Professor of Environmental Science at Washington University, addressed a labor convention in New York City in 1972 on the subject of environmental protection. Afterwards, I went up to him and asked whether he was related to the Kaminer family. He actually remembered the type of candy I used to buy for him.

On my way to work one morning in December 1930, I passed a long line outside the locked doors of a branch of the Bank of the United States on the corner opposite my shop. The customers of the Bank of the U.S. and its branches in various parts of the city were mainly working people and small business owners. The newspaper headlines that day displayed "Throngs Calm as Branches Close." A few days later, the newspaper reported, "Depositors Storm Branch at Southern Boulevard and Freeman Street." Eventually several of the bank's officers were sent to jail and for years afterward a committee of depositors struggled to recover something of their savings when the bank's assets were sold off.

One morning I saw my father leave for a fruit market to buy a wooden crate of apples. He was one of countless thousands of unemployed working people who took up President Herbert Hoover's suggestion to sell apples to tide them over until the "recovery," which was projected to happen within two months. Desperate men crowded the city's street corners, all trying to sell apples to passersby. Long before the sixty days were up, most of the apple sellers, including my father, had surrendered to reality.

In March of 1931, when I was 20 years old, I witnessed my first political demonstration. My employers gave me permission to take an extended lunch hour so that I could ride up from the old elevated station at Chatham Square near Chinatown to Union Square for the demonstration. The press gave extensive coverage to the Communist Party call for nationwide demonstrations to help the unemployed. Although promoters of the demonstration were advocating for jobs and unemployment insurance, many newspapers, such as those owned by William Randolph Hearst, treated the demonstration as a call to revolution.

The municipal authorities gave notice that the entire police force would be used to hold the demonstrators in check. According to press reports, the estimated 110,000 people filling the north end of the square and the surrounding side streets were hemmed in by police. On the rooftops surrounding the square, I viewed the sea of police. Speakers at the demonstration announced they were going to City Hall with a petition asking Mayor Jimmy Walker to help the unemployed, and they invited the crowd to follow. For the police, this was the signal to launch a brutal assault. Mounted police rode into the crowd swinging their clubs, knocking people to the pavement, and pushing their horses into demonstrators. This is how a peaceful meeting turned into a bloody riot.

As a result of the police attack, a delegation that tried to present a petition for unemployment relief to the mayor was arrested and later sentenced to six months in jail "for inciting to riot." Those arrested included Communist Party leaders William Z. Foster, the leader of the 1919 American Federation of Labor (AFL) national steel strike; Robert Minor, onetime cartoonist at the *St. Louis Post-Dispatch;* and Israel Amter, official of the New York Communist Party.

As the Depression worsened, even the buyers of our custom-tailored clothing began purchasing fewer clothes. Eventually, the shop owners laid me off. It was at that time that I became a full-time volunteer working against unemployment while I was seeking other ways of surviving economically. I passed civil service examinations for post office clerk, editorial clerk, courtroom Yiddish interpreter, and customs inspector. I only worked at the post office for one week at Christmas, even though I had earned a very high grade on the examination. My almost perfect grade on the customs inspector test didn't even lead to an interview, and I got no further with the editorial job either. I got some work at the Art Students League as a nude model. Standing or sitting in one position for a whole morning turned out to be much tougher than I expected, but it paid $3 a session—a great sum at that time.

In the early 1930's, the issue of unemployment insurance was gaining momentum. Underemployed and with time on my hands, I went to hear Matthew Woll, president of the Photo Engravers Union and a vice president of the AFL who was speaking in January 1932 at the Rand School, headquarters of the Socialist Party. At the end of his talk, I stood up in the balcony and asked Woll to explain why, at its last two conventions, the AFL had declared against unemployment insurance and had focused instead on repealing Prohibition.

I knew the rationale for this was the expectation that beer brewing and the manufacture of barrels and bottles and other related economic activities would provide stimulus to restore the nation's economy. I tried to question this rationale. But instead of the expected response from Woll, the entire meeting was hastily adjourned by the chairman, Socialist Party officer Algernon Lee. On the way out, I was stopped by the manager of the

Socialist Party bookstore in the building, Jack Altman, who told me that although he agreed with what I said, I should not have challenged Woll.

Despite the opposition of the AFL's national leaders, an independent movement for unemployment insurance won the support of more than 1200 AFL local unions. As late as February 1938, it was estimated that nearly thirteen million Americans were still out of work, and momentum toward passage of unemployment insurance was gathering such force that it could not be stopped.

Several months after I was laid off at the clothing factory, I found a job lugging reels of cable and household electrical appliances for two partners who bought up inventory from bankrupt manufacturers and wholesalers. They resold the goods to hardware stores and other retailers. I earned $15 a week, down $5 from what I made carrying expensive suits for Wall Street.

Every week, I'd come home and drop most of my pay into a cup in the kitchen for my mother to use for the family's needs. Meanwhile, my father was arrested for peddling vegetables from a pushcart without a license. (In fact, no licenses were being issued because neighborhood merchants objected to the competition.) In the summer, he sold ice cream on Coney Island beaches. Years later, he would enjoy recalling his appearances before city magistrates: he would say "Guilty with an explanation, Your Honor." The courtroom was always filled with similar lawbreakers. For nearly a year, my $15 per week was the only money that came regularly into our home.

One evening, my father asked me to accompany him to visit the holder of the second mortgage on our house. There was no money to meet the payments, and foreclosure threatened us as it did countless other homeowners. In a tenement house on the lower east side of Manhattan, my father pleaded with the man not to foreclose. We finally managed to keep our home through these negotiations.

The growth of mass movements in the 1930s against the effects of the Depression led to the election of President Franklin D. Roosevelt and a congress committed to meeting people's immediate needs through the New Deal. For many, however, the collapse of the economy was proof that society itself needed a radical transformation. I grew up accepting my father's conviction that the Socialist Party would be the vehicle to lead society to a better world for working people. I was also drawn at that time to the communist movement because of its efforts on behalf of working people during the Depression.

Several of my Experimental College friends had become members of a Young Communist League (YCL) branch that met at a storefront headquarters on Hicks Street in Brooklyn's Red Hook section. Here, freighters from many parts of the world were loaded and unloaded. I joined the YCL and stopped at their headquarters several evenings a week on the way home after delivering electrical supplies.

Our group made efforts to meet with the surrounding neighbors who were mostly unemployed. We also met with dockworkers. These were usually Italian immigrants. Our conversations with them provided us with material for a little paper dealing with community problems. I volunteered to supervise the writing and production of the paper on a mimeograph machine. Cartoonist Ryan Walker, a nationally known labor artist at the Communist Party's *Daily Worker*, responded to my request for a masthead showing a longshoreman. This was especially meaningful to me because, as a child, I had enjoyed Walker's comic strip in the *New York Call*, a Socialist Party newspaper. The strip was built around a gullible worker called Henry Dubb, the perpetual victim of his greedy boss. Several of Walker's *Call* cartoons were reproduced in Upton Sinclair's *Cry for Justice*, an anthology of social protest literature.

At times, we held our branch meetings in the homes of longshoremen who were wary of being seen entering our storefront. Those regarded as troublemakers by employers could be barred from getting jobs or were even threatened with violent reprisals. Sometimes, as we sat talking about community problems, a prostitute would stop by and go into the bedroom of the man whose apartment we were using. As my knowledge of the oldest profession came from literature, I was surprised to see a demure young woman among the prostitutes.

The way to a waterfront job was to line up every morning and wait to be picked for work by a union official. This was an ideal way of enforcing conformity to the Longshoreman's Association, which was commonly known to be led by the Anastasia gangster mob. Among the longshoremen with whom we worked were members of the Communist Party who had fled Italy under Benito Mussolini. I was reminded again of the perils these men faced when several years later a union organizer named Pete Panto was found murdered, his body weighted down by cement. He was the leader of the rank and file movement that was trying to wrest the longshoremen's union from the mob.

Some of our unemployed members would stand outside a nearby metal bed factory, the Kay Manufacturing Company, to talk to workers when they came out for lunch. Their grievances and needs became material for our paper. The paper also provided information on tactics for fighting unemployment, including advice to workers to join the Steel and Metal Workers Union, formed in 1932.

Several blocks south of our headquarters, there was a huge city garbage dump where homeless people lived in shacks built out of discarded lumber and cardboard boxes. This was one of the numerous "Hoovervilles" around the country, named in honor of the former President. Its residents would scrounge for garbage to eat and for pieces of metal to sell. We gathered stories from the tenants and encouraged them to join us in efforts to eliminate the conditions under which they lived.

Initially, our Young Communist League branch consisted mainly of young Jews, some still in high school, some college dropouts, as well as several unemployed college graduates who came from various parts of the city. As we gained respect in the area, local young unemployed Italians joined us. Some became members and others just came to hear us talk about economic conditions. We were always treated respectfully, despite the radical new ideas we were advancing.

One of the first pieces of legislation enacted by Congress after President Franklin Roosevelt was inaugurated in 1933 was the *Federal Home Owners Loan Act*, which provided low-interest mortgages to replace those held by banks or other private lenders. After my father's death, I found a document entitled, "Loan No. 30-A-38990 to Louis Lerner, Sadie Lerner and James Lerner, his son," for the sum of $3,810. 66. It committed us to paying the federal government the amount of $30.14 every month. Apparently I was included among the parties responsible for the loan because I was the only regular breadwinner at the time.

I still remember the one time my father actually used the house for a political purpose. In 1937, as part of a nationwide campaign to protest Japan's invasion of China, some teenagers were arrested for picketing a Woolworth's store. They were demanding that it stop selling toys made in Japan. My father put up the deed to the house in lieu of bail so that the young demonstrators would not have to spend the night in jail. As for the house, the Depression passed, World War II came and went, and the mortgage payments were finally paid off in the 1940's.

In 1932, I chaired a meeting in which reports were made on various efforts to organize working youth into trade unions. A young woman talked about her job in a factory where she was trying to interest workers in becoming members of the Shoe Workers Union. I sought her out after the meeting and learned that she was a graduate of Hunter College with a major in physics. She found it difficult to find work, like countless others with college degrees. She became convinced that organizing working people was vital to turning the country around. That was how I met my wife, Gertrude Fisher.

In her last year of college, Gertrude took a federal examination for a position as senior mathematician in physics. She received a score of 99 on the math section and 100 in the sections on mechanics and general physics. This placed her fourth on a national list. But there was a catch. Replying to her inquiry about when she might expect to be hired, the United States Civil Service Commission replied on August 29, 1931: "There are separate registers for men and women — greater demand for male eligibles." Six years later, the commission informed hef that her "relative standing" among females was first. Meanwhile, a male friend of hers who had not done as well in the examination had long found professional work.

During World War II, Gertrude looked for work as a physics teacher in New York high schools, where she again held a high place on the "women's list." Every six months, she recalls, a new test was given. But only men were being hired, and the women's list remained untouched. Three "men's lists" were exhausted in this period. She was finally called for an interview by James Madison High School in Brooklyn, New York, for an assignment as "teacher in training." However, the chairman of the physics department greeted her on the first day by telling her he didn't want any women teachers, and that he would refuse to have his department be a test of the separate women's list.

After demanding to know whether she could type, he said he might be able to use her. He then directed her to dust the closets in his office. Gertrude, who went to James Madison High School that day to teach physics, was put to work as a cleaning woman while wearing her best dress. She only broke down when she got home. She subsequently joined a New York Teachers Union that was eventually successful in its efforts to wipe out such degrading practices. At James Madison, she got assigned to teach general science, but was not permitted to teach the subject in which she had shown such promise. At the end of the year as a teacher in training, despite an excellent teaching evaluation, she was terminated.

Gertrude eventually got a job with the Works Progress Administration (WPA), a federal job program during Roosevelt's New Deal. She gathered resources to be used in preparing teaching materials at Lincoln School, an experimental elementary school run by Columbia University. The job included interviewing tugboat captains in New York harbor. By the time Gert had survived the Great Depression, bias against women, and the effect on the teaching profession of the House Un-American Activities Committee hearings under Senator Joseph McCarthy, she never realized her hope to be a physics teacher.

Jim and Gertrude Lerner, newlyweds, 1934.

Gertrude and I married for the first time on October 22, 1934. She had been living in Williamsburg and I was with my parents in Brighton Beach. We met up on our wedding day at the Brooklyn Marriage License Bureau, and asked people waiting in line to serve as witnesses. After the brief ceremony, we both returned to our jobs. Although we were now married, we did not tell anyone except our parents because married women at that time were often not able to get or keep jobs unless they were able to prove they were the sole support of the family. We rented two rooms in my parents' home, paid for by Gert from her $18 weekly salary at the WPA.

A year later, we answered a *New York Times* advertisement for an apartment in Brooklyn Heights. The real estate agent told us, "We don't take niggers, wops, or kikes." Since it would be several decades before a law was enacted barring discrimination in housing, we ended up going from agent to agent. We next started looking in the Flatbush section of Brooklyn in an area that was a short walk from the Brooklyn Dodgers' Ebbets Field. A real estate agent scrolled down a list of available vacancies, at each one repeating, "no Jews."

We then went to yet another real estate office located next to the Cortelyou Road station of the Brighton subway line. We went through yet another long list of rentals indicating "no Jews." The agent finally found a listing for a one-room apartment on East 5th Street where the occupant was anxious to get out of the lease by subletting to us. This became our first residence, and after that, we never left East 5th Street.

Gert and I married again in 1936 in Manhattan so she could acknowledge that she was a married woman when she reported to her job as a high school science teacher. We later bought a permanent home nearby on East 5th Street where our children grew up and where we spent over 65 years of marriage.

A section of the Prospect Expressway was later built in full view of those brick apartment buildings where we had once unsuccessfully looked for our first independent home. Over the years I traveled along that stretch of road endless times, rarely failing to hear "no niggers, wops, or kikes."

PART TWO

American League Against War And Fascism

CHAPTER FOUR

Founding of the American League Against War and Fascism

When I attended the founding congress of the American League Against War and Fascism in New York on September 29, 1933, at age 22, I was aware that a historic international conference against fascism had taken place the year before in Europe. Alarmed by the ongoing international arms race and the advance of fascism in Germany, a distinguished group of labor and political leaders and intellectuals had sponsored a World Congress Against War. It had originally been scheduled for August 27–29, 1932, in Geneva, Switzerland. However, the Swiss government denied permission for the international peace conference to meet in Geneva when it learned that Communist Party representatives from the Soviet Union planned to attend. As a result, the congress was moved to Amsterdam.

Writer Malcolm Cowley put out an appeal for funds to send an American delegation to the Amsterdam congress. The fundraising committee included journalist Lincoln Steffens; novelist John Dos Passos; International Ladies Garment Workers Union leader, Charles Zimmerman; Columbia University anthropologist Franz Boas; and University of Wisconsin professor and poet William Ellery Leonard. Also on the committee were Roger Baldwin, executive secretary of the American Civil Liberties Union (ACLU), and Earl Browder, Communist Party executive secretary.

Sponsors of the Amsterdam conference included scientist Albert Einstein and novelists Thomas Mann of Germany, Romain Rolland and Henri Barbusse of France, Maxim Gorky of the Soviet Union, Martin Anderson-Nexo for the Scandinavian countries, and the Irish playwright George

Bernard Shaw. Also among the sponsors were Cesar Agostino Sandino, the Nicaraguan general who was leading guerrilla battles in Nicaragua against the United States Marines, and Mme. Sun Yat Sen, whose late husband was the first president of the Chinese republic. She herself was active in the struggle against the Japanese invasion of northern China in 1931–32. The presence of Sandino and Sun Yat Sen was a sign that the peace movement was no longer limited to the international pacifist peace organizations.[3]

Professor H. W. L. Dana of the United States made a point to report to the delegates at Amsterdam that the American delegation of 32 people was primarily a workers' delegation, including representatives of American metal workers, machinists, marine workers, carpenters, textile workers, ex-service men, men and women from different parts of the country and different racial backgrounds, and different classes and political perspectives. Also present from the United States were representatives of the Rabbinical Assembly of America; the Fellowship of Reconciliation; the Women's Peace Society; and the Women's International League for Peace and Freedom (WILPF).[4]

Following the Amsterdam meeting, three American authors — Sherwood Anderson, Theodore Dreiser, and Upton Sinclair — initiated the call for a congress against fascism in the United States. Meanwhile, Adolf Hitler's assumption of power in Germany in January 1933 made the threat of war even more ominous. Emerging out of these prefiguring events, the first American Congress Against War and Fascism took place on September 29 to October 1, 1933, in New York City. The list of supporting organizations and individuals read like a "who's who" in the struggle for national unemployment insurance and social security, and included the new labor movement that was rapidly growing among the industrial workforce. Similar to the World Congress in Amsterdam, representatives came from across a very wide and diverse spectrum.

Other sponsors of the founding congress included leaders of WILPF, the pacifist War Resisters League, the Women's Peace Society, World Peaceways, Inc., the People's Lobby (headed by philosopher John Dewey), as well as the Communist Party and the League for Industrial Democracy, an organization influenced by the Socialist Party, that was especially prominent among intellectuals. The support of this national peace movement by the Communist and Socialist Parties carried special weight at that time because in the 1932 presidential elections, socialist Norman Thomas won 900,000 votes and communist William Z. Foster received 100,000 votes.

Several weeks before the 1933 congress was to assemble, the new American peace movement had experienced its first crisis when the National Executive Committee of the Socialist Party announced it was withdrawing from the organizing committee. The Socialists accused the Communist Party newspaper the *Daily Worker* of making "vicious attacks" on the Socialist Party. The two parties had been at loggerheads, almost since the founding of the Communist Party USA following the First World War.

For some time, Communist Party leaders had been seeking to enlist the support of Socialist Party members for the peace movement while at the same time engaging in criticism of the history and policies of the Socialist Party. When the socialists decided to withdraw from the preparations for the antiwar congress, Party leaders cited, among other reasons, an article in the *Daily Worker* (July 29, 1933) that appeared a couple of months prior to the upcoming congress. Under the headline "Socialist Party Deceives Workers," it accused the Party's leaders of distracting workers from the antiwar movement by implying that the war in Europe was not likely to directly affect Americans.

In its withdrawal announcement, the Socialist Party stated that Robert Minor, a Communist Party spokesman on the congress arrangements committee, had pledged that accusations of this kind against the socialists would not continue to be put forth. The leaders of the Socialist Party therefore charged a breach of faith and withdrew their organization from the organizing committee. Many members of the Socialist Party sent a telegram urging their party's executive committee to reconsider the decision to withdraw, but to no avail. Despite this dissension among their ranks, many Socialist Party members, including entire New York City branches, remained associated with the American League Against War and Fascism and participated in the congress.

More than 2600 delegates from 35 states attended the public meetings of the League's first congress at New York City's St. Nicholas Arena on West 66th Street, and the Mecca Temple on West 56th Street. The St. Nicholas Arena public meeting was chaired by Joseph B. Matthews, a member of the Socialist Party and former missionary in Asia who had presided over a World Youth Peace Congress in Holland in 1928. He was incumbent executive secretary of the pacifist Fellowship of Reconciliation. Matthews seemed an ideal choice to direct an organization intended to bring together labor and religious groups, working people, and professionals. Reinhold Niebuhr, professor of Applied Christianity at Union Theological Seminary, was permanent chair of the congress sessions. [5]

In the audience were people who rarely if ever found common ground. These included representatives of the Farmers Holiday Association, a group formed in the Midwest during the Depression. Their program consisted of resistance to evictions and bank foreclosures, by force, or by withholding of crops or payments (called "holiday"), if necessary. Other groups, whose purpose was to advocate resistance to war through nonviolent measures, included members of the Fellowship of Reconciliation, the Women's Peace Union, and supporters of the national cooperative movement. Many who were active in the movement for unemployment insurance also were present. An organization of veterans of the First World War also attended.

An indication of the impressive diverse nature of the congress could be clearly seen in its souvenir journal. Advertisements promoted the Methodist Federation for Social Service; *The Nation* magazine; WILPF; the Women's Peace Society; the noncommunist Conference for Progressive Labor Action; the War Resisters League; the Workers and Farmers Cooperative Unity Alliance of Superior, Wisconsin; the communist *Daily Worker;* and the socialist League for Industrial Democracy.

Speakers at the opening session of the congress included Harriet Stanton Blatch, prominent feminist and pacifist; Emil Rieve, president of the American Federation of Hosiery Workers; William Pickens, field secretary of the National Association for the Advancement of Colored People (NAACP); Henri Barbusse, chairman of the World Committee for

Struggle Against Fascism; Alphonse Goldschmidt, exiled former professor of economics at the University of Leipzig; Communist Party secretary Earl Browder; A. J. Muste, a pacifist and chairman of the Conference for Progressive Labor Action; pacifist Devere Allen; and William N. Jones, editor of the *Baltimore Afro-American.*

At the conclusion of the congress, Joseph P. Matthews was chosen permanent chairman of the League. William Pickens and Earl Browder became vice-chairmen, and two secretaries were later chosen by the officers to direct the organization's day-to-day operations. One of them, Donald Henderson, had lost a teaching position at Columbia University for espousing causes that Nicholas Murray Butler, its president, objected to as "communistic" in origin. Francis M. Henson, the other secretary, was at that time executive secretary of the National Religion and Labor Foundation, and a member of the Socialist Party. He had been a labor organizer among West Virginia coal miners.

Historically, peace organizations had appealed to more narrow constituencies. Some organizations specifically based their opposition to war on religious grounds according to their particular faith; some organizations were pacifists opposed to capitalism but committed to changing society by peaceful means; and several directed their organizing efforts only to women. Among these were the leaders of the successful crusade for women's suffrage that culminated in the ratification of the *Nineteenth Amendment to the Constitution* in 1919.

Several months after its birth, the new American League Against War and Fascism became one of 43 international affiliates of the World Committee Against War and Fascism headed by Lord Robert Cecil of Great Britain and Pierre Cot, a prominent French Socialist.

Pacifists were conflicted over whether they could cooperate with communists, who held that wars of liberation from colonialism and capitalism were justified. Devere Allen, a prominent pacifist who edited the journal *The World Tomorrow,* urged pacifists to adopt a policy of "passive resistance" to war. After attending the New York congress on behalf of WILPF's international office in Geneva, another pacifist, Emily Greene Balch, recommended cooperation with the American League "without blurring our own position ... this cooperation gives us chances to express our conviction that resort to violence hinders, instead of helps, the coming of a more just economic society." (*Rosika* Schwimmer Peace Collection at the New York Public Library).

Despite the unprecedented breadth of participation in the antiwar and antifascist efforts beginning in the early 1930's, it should be remembered that the League consistently sustained awareness of its historic connections to previous protest movements, including associations with Eugene V. Debs and the Socialist Party and Earl Browder of the Communist Party. The League counted among its officers and members many men and women who were conscientious objectors or crusaders against capitalism during the First World War. Many had lost their jobs or served prison terms. Earl Browder was sentenced to two years in the federal penitentiary at Leavenworth at the age of twenty-six for his opposition to the war. Roger Baldwin, head of the ACLU, received a year's sentence for refusing to register for the draft. New espionage laws at that time made speeches, leaflets, and newspaper articles against the war equivalent to treason.

In pursuit of its organizational goal of becoming a unifying force with a program that other organizations could accept, the League's founders set up a plan for national and local affiliations. It would establish a network of League chapters composed of individual members who would make opposition to war their principal activity.

Coast to Coast

After I went to the public rally in September 1933 that welcomed delegates to the founding congress of the American League Against War and Fascism, I headed straight to the League's office to offer my assistance in building its youth division. As a reference, I mentioned my membership in the Young Communist League since it was one of the League's founding organizations. My offer was immediately accepted by the office secretary who I soon learned did not even have enough money for postage. Nevertheless, I quit my job for $15 a week at the electrical supply business on the lower west side of New York City and began devoting myself exclusively to organizing, writing and speaking on behalf of the League.

About 500 young people had come as delegates to the founding congress. I personally called on some of them who lived in the New York City area to help set up the Youth Section. Our extremely low dues were inadequate for meeting expenses, so we began making frequent appeals for contributions. Minutes of the League's "National Bureau" dated December 3, 1934, state: "Recommendation by the organizing committee that $15 per week be put in the national office budget for the Youth Section organizer to be paid if and when we can raise it." That, of course, referred to me.[6]

It was part of the League's plan to build local organizations around the country that would be concerned not only with its national program but also with local legislative and community issues bearing on peace and democratic rights. Following the League's founding congress in New York, delegates initiated local, statewide, and regional conferences. In the Los Angeles area, hundreds of people filled the Orange Grove Theater to form a branch of the League. Among the organizations represented at this meeting were the War Resisters League, the Fellowship of Reconciliation, Methodist Churches, the Socialist and Communist Parties, and the National Student League. [7]

One month later, at a meeting in San Francisco, delegates from 30 cities formed another regional organization of the League. Their efforts included large gatherings at churches and homes in the Bay Area. One of these took place at the home of John Galen Howard, renowned architect of the University of California at Berkeley campus, whose wife was an officer in the local League chapter. [8]

In March, 1934, at a convention of the International Longshoremen's Association (ILA),[9] delegates voted to recommend that all of the union's locals refuse to load or unload any ship flying the Nazi flag. A few days later on March 14, 1934, despite threats of violence by the American Silver Shirts, a national Nazi organization, more than 7,000 anti-war protestors gathered in Los Angeles. The defense of labor rights, free speech, and other civil rights were a major part of all of the western meetings and actions against impending world war.

A year later, on April 6, 1935, delegates from almost 200 organizations met in Seattle on the 17th anniversary of American entrance into World War I. They established a northwest section of the League that was committed to building branches in Idaho, Washington, and Oregon. The meeting reflected the dramatic upsurge in the labor movement, especially on the Pacific coast, after the 1934 general strike that followed the murder of two workers. Representatives of more that two dozen locals of the AFL sat alongside members of the Baptist Young People's Union, the Socialist and Communist Parties, and various independent political movements.

The meeting in Seattle was followed on April 27-28, 1935, by the first Pacific Coast Congress Against War and Fascism in San Francisco. The fact that it was held at the Building Trades Council reflected the strong sponsorship of the meeting by trade unions. Officers of the Boilermakers Union and the Longshoremen addressed the congress. In addition to League and labor representatives, other organizations included the Democratic Party, California State Federation of Colored Women's Clubs, and the Communist Party.[10] Immediately following the San Francisco meetings, tours for speakers were set up to establish a network of local League committees across the northwest. Not all conferences and meetings to establish League organizations carried through on their initial enthusiasm. Many met, made plans, and elected officers, but were unable to maintain a permanent organization.[11]

The Magazine

Immediately after its founding in November 1933, the League began publishing a monthly magazine, *The Fight Against War and Fascism.* It sold at the subscription rate of 50 cents a year. People commonly referred to it as *Fight*, inevitably causing some discomfort among the many pacifists in the League. The editor, Joseph Pass, was not new to opposing war. He and his artist brother, Morris, both members of the Young People's Socialist League, were among four men sentenced to a year in prison in Seattle during World War I for writing and speaking against the draft.

Joseph Pass came to journalism after working for three years in the Yukon where he served as a fireman on river boats. He befriended Indians and gold prospectors who had lost their illusions of getting rich. His early experiences reporting on labor strikes also helped make him an ideal editor for an organization that proposed to bring together the American people into an antiwar movement. He was also a *raconteur* for those of us who shared office space with him.

Pass set up an editorial committee that included Malcolm Cowley and Joseph P. Lash of the Student League for Industrial Democracy. Pass solicited articles and art from his many friends in the radical cultural movement centered around the John Reed Club, named after the author of *Ten Days That Shook the World*, the famous firsthand account of the Russian Revolution. Art Young, the leading labor and socialist cartoonist of the time, also contributed to *Fight*. It was always understood that no one received payment for their writing or art work for the magazine.[12]

Fight soon became a 32 page, five-color periodical. It reflected how government-sponsored work programs during the Depression had created ties between the art and literary worlds and millions of working people. The first issue included articles by famed French novelist Henri Barbusse and poet Langston Hughes. Hughes wrote about recent race riots in Chicago, Washington, and St. Louis.[13]

Commenting on Hitler's takeover of the German government early in 1933, Joseph P. Matthews, Chairman of the League's founding congress, wrote that there was an ever present threat that some eventual combination of European powers would make war against the Soviet Union. So influential was the longstanding opposition to the Soviet Union in the United States that it had only recently been officially recognized as a nation by President Roosevelt, 16 years after the Russian revolution. Groups on the left within the new peace movement were very alarmed that governmental alliances developing in Europe might lead to war against the Soviet Union.

The communists who played an important part in establishing the League persuaded many pacifists and others at the founding congress to adopt a program expressing concern over threatened war against the Soviet Union, and other threats to peace elsewhere in Europe, Latin America, and Asia. *Fight* reported that Matthews had gone to Cuba to investigate American intervention there after President Roosevelt dispatched 30 American warships to Cuba in the fall of 1933 to protect American property. This was a reaction to the seizure of American-owned sugar mills by Cuban workers who were protesting employment conditions. American investments in Cuba at that time amounted to more than $1.5 billion.

In December, 1933, several weeks after the League was formed and while living in Carmel, California, 30-year-old poet Langston Hughes participated in an antiwar rally sponsored by the Peninsula American League Against War and Fascism. Two years later, Hughes addressed the First Pacific Coast Congress Against War and Fascism in San Francisco in April 1935. He also collaborated with Ella Winters on the play *Blood on the Fields*, a study of violent attacks on American farm workers who were attempting to build a union. His support of the antiwar movement and exploited farm workers brought Hughes threats on his life. (See *The Life of Langston Hughes* by Arnold Rampersad, Oxford, 2 volumes, 1986, 1988).

On inauguration day, March 4, 1933, ten days after assuming office, President Roosevelt proposed several measures for dealing with unemployment, including the establishment of a Civilian Conservation Corps (CCC) to restore and maintain parks and forests. The CCC enrolled 400,000 young men between the ages of 17 and 23 at an annual pay of $360. After operation of the camps was assigned to the U.S. War Department, the peace movement became alarmed that the camps might be used to militarize youth, as was happening with such camps in other countries. This concern increased when Assistant Secretary of War Woodring stated that the camp mobilization "was the first real test of the army's plans for war mobilization."

The official newspaper of the camps, *Happy Days CCC*, claimed that "no training can possibly be of more advantage to the reforestation men than military training." Similarly, the *New York Daily News*, the country's largest newspaper, described the camps as a military organization without guns, and suggested that all of the young men in the CCC be placed in the military reserves.

When I found out that a bill was already in Congress to make the camps a permanent institution, I called this to the attention of the League. We also learned that *Happy Days* was advocating the requirement of one compulsory year in a CCC camp for every boy reaching the age of 18 or high school graduation. The League therefore began arguing that it would be much better if young people learned trades and had access to jobs at living wages. If jobs were not available, the League proposed that a system of unemployment insurance be established.

Editor Pass invited me to write a column for *Fight* called "Youth Speaks." In January 1934, I reported in my first column that a student subcommittee of the League sought to abolish part of the War Department, the Reserve Officers Training Corps (ROTC), and that we were already circulating petitions to that effect.

A delegation of 20 people headed by Chairman Matthews arranged to meet with government officials in Washington, D.C. on January 19, 1934, to advance the views of the League on the administration's armaments policies. This first action in Washington represented the League's hopes to build an all-inclusive peace movement. Similar meetings were scheduled to take place simultaneously in 25 cities.[14] Our League delegation to Washington drove all night from the Theater Union building on 14th Street in Manhattan to the nation's capitol. Two of my companions rode in the enclosed front seats, while I squeezed into the open air rumble seat and covered myself with a blanket for protection against the January snowstorm.

At the Washington headquarters of WILPF, Eleanor Fowler, the organization's labor secretary, helped the delegation arrange appointments with various government officials. All of them were either noncommittal, discouraging, or antagonistic. "Write us a letter," said President Roosevelt's secretary when Matthews proposed that instead of building up the armed forces, money should be spent to establish a national system of unemployment and social insurance.[15]

Civilian Conservation Corps Director Robert Fechner rejected outright our proposal that the conservation camps be taken away from army control. He claimed that William Green, president of the AFL, was in agreement. This was not surprising because Green stood in the mold of his predecessor Samuel Gompers who had been a staunch supporter of U.S. participation in World War I. Green was also known to oppose unemployment insurance and social security. Speaker of the House, Henry T. Rainey, told our delegation he expected war between Japan and the Soviet Union by spring. This prediction was consistent with news reports that Japanese armies, which had invaded Manchuria, were approaching the Soviet border.

Heading for home the next night by bus, I went sleepless for a second straight night when the heating system on the bus broke down and its engine gave up outside Wilmington, Delaware. When we finally made it back to New York City, I fell asleep on the subway and awoke to discover that the car I was on was traveling in the wrong direction.

In the six years of its existence, the CCC went on to enroll 2,200,000 young men between the ages of 17 and 23, but it was never turned into a military organization. It accomplished much valuable work, especially in restoring forests. It was reported that during its existence the corps planted 1,855,000,000 trees. It is difficult, of course, to know how much influence the youth and peace movements had in keeping the CCC from being turned into a military project, but I believe our opposition to its militarization influenced the outcome.

I began receiving invitations to speak about the League's program to young people around New York City. When I addressed the student body at Abraham Lincoln High School in Brooklyn in February 1934, the auditorium was filled with students. It brought home to me the fact that growing numbers of young people were becoming acutely aware of the threat of impending war and how it could affect them.

Some pacifists, including Jessie Wallace Hughan of the War Resisters League (WRL), continued to see the League Against War and Fascism as a valuable organization for building opposition to war. In an article for *Fight*, Hughan wrote that although the League "works indefatigably to educate the American people in the economic causes of war," WRL was nevertheless reluctant to accept the League as "the mass anti-war movement" that WRL had been seeking as far back as 1914. This reticence was not because they regarded the League as too radical. "We recognize with the League that capitalism, fascism and war stand together," she wrote. However, she strongly criticized the League for its failure to adopt a policy of total opposition to all wars.

Responding in the same issue of the magazine, Paul Reid, who had been named Executive Secretary of the League early in 1934, emphasized that the presence of pacifists in the League was evidence that the organization "provides a rallying ground" for people and organizations who were united in common resistance to war. Reid argued that those who were convinced that individual resistance to war was the correct path to peace, and those who were just as strongly convinced that only a radical change of society toward socialism was the correct path, would all be welcome under the League's program.

The League's officers had hoped that such issues as disarmament, opposition to U.S. policies in Latin America, restrictions on democratic rights, and the international sales of war materials would transcend the disputes over pacifism. However, for some peace organizations, the League's refusal to condemn all wars, including those that would be fought by the Spanish Republic or by the Chinese people against the Japanese invaders, was a barrier not only to their membership in the League but also to engaging in any joint peace actions. Frederick J. Libby of the National Council for Prevention of War, formed in 1921 to coordinate the efforts of a number of peace organizations, declared that it was impossible "to find sufficient grounds for cooperation with a committee that includes communists." Even within some pacifist organizations, the Spanish Republic's stalwart resistance to fascism led to differences among members over their pledge of nonviolence in all circumstances.

Communists and Socialists Fall Out

Several weeks after our first lobbying efforts in Washington, D.C. in 1934, the American League Against War and Fascism suffered a severe setback when some members from the League for Industrial Democracy unexpectedly resigned. The resignation was announced in a statement issued by the League's executive committee in the April 1934 issue of *Fight*. Those who left the League included its chairman, Joseph P. Matthews, and one of the two League secretaries, Francis M. Henson. Both were Socialist Party members who had personally remained with the American League despite their party's withdrawal on the eve of the first congress in 1933. It was well-known that the Communist Party and Socialist Party were always on edge in relationship to each other because of longstanding and deep conflicts over ideological and organizing issues. Now, however, Matthews and Henson were resigning from the League because of an incident that furthered the deteriorating relationship between the two parties.

Reports from Vienna told of Austrian troops shelling Socialist Party headquarters in several cities. The government outlawed the party and dismissed all municipal officeholders who were members. The renowned cooperative apartment houses in Vienna, one of the Party's greatest achievements, were bombed by government forces and thousands of people were seized and thrown into prison. In New York City, the Communist Party sponsored a demonstration led by Robert Minor, a member of its national committee. The demonstration took place across the street from the Austrian consulate on the corner of Fifth Avenue and 43nd Street. I joined several thousand angry people in defiance of orders by the New York police to disperse. Afterwards, I retained a disturbing image of police beating a tattoo on Minor's uncovered, bald head.

The disputed incident between the socialists and communists that caused the withdrawal of the Socialist Party from the League occurred at a Madison Square Garden meeting called by the Socialist Party to protest the Austrian government's actions. Clarence Hathaway, a Communist Party leader and the Communist Party's spokesman at the League, was severely injured (*New York Times*, February 12, 1934) when he approached the platform amidst noisy bedlam emerging from various parts of the huge arena.

The socialists interpreted the disorder in the hall and Hathaway's advance toward the platform as an intentional effort by communists to take over the meeting. For this reason, people on the platform physically pushed Hathaway away and he sustained a head injury. This incident was widely publicized in the press. With his head still bandaged, Hathaway visited the League's office. He tried to explain that his only intent in approaching the platform was to prevent Communist Party members, who felt they had been excluded from the Madison Square Garden meeting, from disrupting the event. Whatever the causes of the incident, it was too late to avoid an even more open rift with the Socialist Party. This event was to have longstanding effects.

Members of the League for Industrial Democracy, who belonged to the Socialist Party, but had disagreed with that party's earlier withdrawal from the League's founding committee, now changed their minds and announced that they would no longer work alongside communists in the peace movement. Although the League had nothing to do with the fracas at Madison Square Garden, the incident caused a major setback in our attempts to build a unified peace movement.[16]

A year after Matthews resigned as League chairman, the office received a letter from him expressing his gratification at the "growing support" for the League by the American people. He offered again to help build the movement against war and fascism. He accepted an invitation to rejoin the organization's executive committee, which was led at that time by the new chairman, Dr. Harry F. Ward, professor of Christian Ethics at Union Theological Seminary.

Matthews' second stint at the League was not much longer than his first, and his departure less honorable. A local of the Technical, Editorial and Office Assistants, an affiliate of the AFL, sent a letter dated July 9, 1935, to Paul Reid, the League's executive secretary, asking that the League "take some action on the position of J. B. Matthews." The letter claimed that, as vice-president of the company Consumers Research, Matthews was refusing to recognize their employee union, which at that time was engaged in a strike against the company. According to the union, he was subjecting workers to strikebreaking activities, including hiring men to physically assault them. They further claimed that Matthews had ignored National Labor Relations Board (NLRB) charges that Consumers Research was guilty of violating the *Labor Disputes Act.* The League's officers invited Matthews to give his view of the charges in the letter.

Instead, he submitted his resignation to the League on the grounds that he wanted to spare it any "embarrassment" caused by the dispute.[17]

Frustrated in their dealings with Matthews, the Consumers Research strikers left to form the highly successful Consumers Union. Matthews later became known as one of the most notorious informers for the House Un-American Activities Committee (HUAC) against his former associates in peace, religious and socialist organizations. He even became the Committee's research director, and briefly held a similar position in the early 1950s with Senator Joseph McCarthy's office.

Matthews' second resignation from the League had little effect on its work. Following the split in leadership over developments in Austria, League officers dedicated themselves to overcoming divisions that were endangering the organization's very survival. They emphasized the League's growth since its founding five months earlier. Highly successful conferences were held in Chicago, San Francisco, Boston, and many smaller cities. A series of student antiwar conferences took place at Columbia University, and other regional conferences involved student groups from scores of universities. The League sent a delegation to the opening of the U.S. Congress to oppose the war budget. Large demonstrations and parades against Austrian fascism were held under the auspices of the League in Chicago and Pittsburgh.

The new League chairman, Dr. Harry F. Ward, was a British-born graduate of Northwestern University who earned a master's degree from Harvard before settling down near the Chicago stockyards as a Methodist minister. For eight years, he directed the activities of a church that served packing house workers during the time Upton Sinclair was doing research in the stockyards for his book, *The Jungle*. Ward closely followed the problems of stockyard workers and participated in their difficult and often dangerous efforts to organize a union. He was committed to religion to the extent that it worked to improve social and economic conditions.[18]

League organizers found that they could get sympathetic hearings from clergymen inspired by Ward. Sometimes it was sufficient for me merely to mention that Harry Ward was the League's chairman to recruit members. The membership of the League's national committee reflected

Ward's standing among both Christian and Jewish religious leaders. This broadening of the League's national leadership had the effect of greater active participation throughout the organization.

I was invited to attend a meeting at Union Theological Seminary where, after a session about the League's purposes, students formed their own branch. This led in January 1936 to an Inter-Seminary movement representing thirty-five different seminaries affiliated with the League. After graduation, many of their students could be found in our branches around the country.

Ward's leadership always proved invaluable. He made young people feel comfortable working at all levels of the organization. When I visited his home in the Palisades on the New Jersey side of the Hudson River, musician and songwriter Earl Robinson was there playing the piano and singing excerpts from his work in progress, *Ballad for Americans*.[19]

The secretary of the League's Women's Committee, Dorothy McConnell, had a strong commitment to expand the League's influence among women. She represented the League at international women's conferences in Europe and Latin America and wrote pamphlets and articles. In one of her pamphlets, *Women, War and Fascism* (December 1935), she urged that a special effort be made to win women over to the antiwar movement. Equal pay for equal work later became the theme for a women's commission set up at the League's 1935 congress.[20]

In August of 1934, I attended the founding convention of the Canadian League Against War and Fascism's youth section in Toronto. The Canadian League, like the American League, was an affiliate of the World Congress founded at Amsterdam. Knowing that I would be put up by members in their homes, I hitchhiked to Toronto. When I travelled from Toronto to Chicago in September of 1934 to help prepare for the second League congress, I wrote Gertrude to tell her that three friends of mine from the Experimental College at Madison, who had moved into a large five-room apartment in Chicago, were away on vacation and that the place "is left for me and another fellow from New York. I wish you could be here now."[21]

American League Against War and Fascism demonstration in Harlem, May 30, 1935.

Organizing for the Congress went fairly well. We received word that off-duty members of five National Guard companies were going to attend, ten Negro youth clubs also planned to send delegates, and we were beginning to get delegates from industrial shops. These successes were due to the commitment of local League supporters, who provided us with the names of organizations to be approached and of specific people who could help with detailed organizing work. The growing number of invitations we received to provide speakers reflected widespread concern over the rise of Hitler in Germany. The amount of support we were now receiving brought home to us as nothing else before, that building the peace movement was worth our unending work and personal sacrifices.

CHAPTER FIVE

Second League Congress and Aftermath

Over 3000 delegates attended the fall 1934 Congress Against War and Fascism. About 750 of them were between the ages of 16 and 25 years old. A spirited public meeting filled the Chicago Coliseum nearly to its capacity of 22,000 people. For the first time, the League's basic organizational structure appeared to be solid. In his report to the delegates, League chairman Harry F. Ward announced that "for the first time in American history, groups which heretofore had no contact with working class movements are working shoulder to shoulder...." He urged forbearance in understanding each other's views.

Ward addressed the disquiet expressed by many conference participants about the possibility that the Communist Party might end up controlling the national organization. Ward emphasized that it had become increasingly impossible for any political party to dominate the League. He assured delegates that when incidents occurred where "zeal outruns knowledge," they were promptly addressed by the National Committee. He reported that several such interventions had already occurred, and asked all political groups to stay focused on the League's principal purpose to prevent war and fascism.

It became evident that negative attitudes around the communist movement had to be overcome if there was to be an effective, unified movement against war. An example of such attitudes was a derisive statement about pacifists that appeared in the *Western Worker*, a Communist newspaper that reported on the Bay Region Congress Against War and Fascism in Berkeley, California, on January 29, 1934. The meeting was attended by 147 organizations. The *Western Worker* reported that "throughout the conference, the pacifist speakers were exposed in their true role of phrase-mongerers with nothing to offer...." (February 12, 1934). This was unfortunately all too reminiscent of the dispute caused by Communist Party rhetoric that led to the Socialist Party's wholesale withdrawal from the League the previous summer.

Besides confirming Methodist minister Harry F. Ward as chairman, the delegates at the 1934 Congress chose three vice-chairmen: Dr. Robert Morss Lovett, president of the League for Industrial Democracy, journalist Lincoln Steffens, and Communist Party leader Earl Browder. From a general denunciation of war and fascism, the League congress in Chicago went on to spell out a program for dealing with antidemocratic tendencies at home. These tendencies included increasing antisemitism, repression of black people, attacks on the growing labor movement, and "the awakening of those hatreds which have for more than a decade gone on in the anti-red hunt in this country." One effort that emerged from the congress was to persuade the American people to realize that fascism could happen here.

After meeting jointly in Chicago with the congress as a whole, the younger participants held separate sessions as the Youth Congress Against War and Fascism. They focused on militarism on campuses and unemployment among youth. This youth congress grew out of the fact that a million college students had gone through the ROTC in the decade ending 1931. Simultaneously, 117,000 young men were put through compulsory military training. During the previous year, more than 75 student antiwar conferences had taken place. Over 30 of them had voted to affiliate with the American League Against War and Fascism.

One of the delegates who spoke at the Chicago youth conference was Walter Petrasky, a textile worker from Pawtucket, Rhode Island. He had just gone through a textile workers' strike, in which workers were victims of excessive violence. The strike spread over several states, and 15 workers had been killed by National Guard units. Although many at the conference had undoubtedly heard about the widely-reported strike, this first-hand description of the brutal attack on workers led to a hushed silence.

Petrasky urged that efforts be made to persuade members of the National Guard not to attack striking workers, The delegate who was chairing that session, read a letter he had just received from a group of National Guardsmen who were attending the convention. The letter stated that "several companies in the National Guard have verbally endorsed your program against strike duty.... We workers in uniform are with you." The letter, greeted with great applause, was signed, "Guardsmen, 33rd Division, Ill. Nat. Guard."

At Chicago, I was elected national chairman of the League's youth section. Until then, I had served in that capacity by appointment. The League's elected national youth committee at that time included people from an array of organizations ranging from the traditional left groups to labor unions and churches.[22]

One of the League's organizing efforts after the Chicago congress took place at the port of Baltimore, where League members boarded ships to distribute pamphlets and conduct discussions on its antiwar program with merchant seamen. In Seattle, a local antiwar movement that included socialist, communist, and church organizations, demonstrated outside a dance hall to protest rising military appropriations. The location was chosen because the captain of a naval training ship was there at the time being entertained.

Many incidents could serve as examples of how difficult it often was for the League to keep its antiwar focus among its widespread branches. All branches of the League had been advised by the national office that, in order to concentrate its efforts on antiwar issues, it was against the organization's policy to participate in May Day labor demonstrations. Nevertheless, when I arrived in Dayton, Ohio, on the eve of May 1, 1935, I was handed a leaflet announcing that James Lerner would be speaking at a May Day demonstration as a representative of the American League Against War and Fascism. Except for my identification and a single line, "Against War and Fascism! All war Funds for the Unemployed!," the entire leaflet dealt with problems of labor in Dayton and unemployment insurance. I spoke at the rally only long enough to state the League's specific antiwar program. And despite national policy that only pamphlets published by the League itself could be sold at its branches or at League meetings, local branches continued to be unclear as to whether to allow the sale of publications of the Communist Party and other organizations.

Earl Browder, the Communist Party's representative on the League's national bureau, assured League officers that the bureau would again advise local organizations that only our literature should be sold or distributed at meetings called by the League (*American League Bureau Minutes*, July 1, 1935). The national officers had to deal with the fact that some League members were advocating a specific Communist Party goal, the building of a national labor party. The League notified its branches (August 5, 1935) that "the League does not concern itself with any labor or political party, and is not to be used in any political maneuvers."

Shacks and Mansions

Although my primary responsibility was building and directing the work of the League's youth section, there was no real separation from the rest of the organization's activities. Working mainly in the eastern half of the country between 1933 and 1939, I traveled locally by cars driven by volunteer members. Between cities, I usually went by bus, rail, and by hitch-hiking. Sometimes when I traveled I stayed in a YMCA or a modest hotel, but generally I found haven in the home of a League member. Beds, cots, sofas, or floors, even if physically uncomfortable, offered an opportunity to spend a few hours with like-minded people. Even when I didn't know where I would be sleeping until the last meeting of the evening, I always preferred this to a hotel room.

During a trip to Ohio in 1935 to seek labor union support for the anti-war movement, I met with the Central Labor Union of Barberton, Ohio, which voted to endorse the American League. I also met with officials of the newly formed United Rubber Workers Union in Akron. In addition, I assembled a group of people who voted to set up a League branch. Inspired by these successes, I moved on to Dayton to seek the support of the head of the AFL.

I also was asked to assist existing branches on the campuses of Cornell University and Syracuse University and to set up other branches further west. I arrived in Rochester with only $5 in my pocket, with Buffalo, New York and Eire, Pennsylvania still ahead. I again wrote home and asked Gert: "If you get this before Friday and can mail a letter so that I get it Saturday, SOS send some money." I confessed to Gert that "this has been my hardest trip to go through. I keep counting the hours actually when I'll see you again. Every once in a while I feel like jumping the tracks and going right back home, but then — war and fascism."

In some geographic areas, such as Rochester, New York, some 300 miles west of New York City, where the Eastman Kodak Company was the main economic force, we had very few leads to potential members. In such cases, I would seek people or local groups whose national organizations or leaders were already supporting the League. Sometimes I would ring doorbells and make telephone calls to people I didn't know, but I found it more productive to make the rounds to rabbis, lawyers, professors, ministers, and union officials. I finally left Rochester confident that a new League branch would be formed there.

When I was moving through the Midwest in the 1930s engaged in organizing against war, I arrived in Cleveland on the day the Fisher Body plant went out on strike," I wrote Gert: "I went out to the plant and saw the sit-downers inside. Wives outside handing in their kids to be kissed by their fathers. Food being handed in or hoisted up in baskets; also, radios, checkers, and handballs...." I was witnessing working people taking part in the greatest organizational movement in United States history. Literally millions of people were forming labor unions.

Defying a Nazi Warship

In 1935, I also spent several weeks in Baltimore with one of the most active branches of the League. The branch was established at a conference on November 2, 1935, attended by representatives of several large labor unions, the League of Women Voters, Christian Endeavor, Protestant and Jewish clergymen, the National Urban League, and the YMCA. It was also attended by businessmen prominent in community affairs and journalists, including *Baltimore Sun* editor Mauritz Hallgren, who also wrote for *Fight*. At a separate session of young people led by the Reverend John Hutchison (former student of Dr. Harry F. Ward at the Union Theological Seminary), members of every Protestant denomination in the area as well as representatives of labor unions and student organizations discussed crime, unemployment, militarism in the high schools and colleges, and discrimination against black youth.

The Baltimore branch led by Sam Swerdloff, an artist in his mid-twenties, developed a creative way of building the peace movement. After selecting a block on which to work, a committee went from house to house getting signatures for a petition to close the street. If this could be done for a carnival, why not for a peace meeting? Once a permit was granted by the City, League members strung lights across the street, set up loudspeakers, and held demonstrations. These gatherings drew as many as twenty-five hundred people at a time.

Since Baltimore was the second-largest U.S. port for the shipment of war materials to Italy and Japan, the Baltimore branch of the League urged local longshoremen to refuse to load war goods. Reverend Joseph S. Nowak, a 1934 graduate of Union Theological Seminary, was put in charge of a mission at St. Paul's Presbyterian Church in Baltimore, known for conducting soap box meetings on the waterfront. He addressed the mostly Polish and black dock workers gathered for the morning's job assignments. Nowak spoke in Polish while I spoke in English. The men hired for the day's work walked by, for the most part without indicating what they thought of our cause to refuse war cargo. However, we became aware that there was almost no indication of the animosity that we sometimes experienced elsewhere toward our antiwar work.

The following spring a newspaper story appeared in the Baltimore press heralding the arrival of the Nazi warship *Emden*. It carried German naval cadets on a "goodwill mission." *The Baltimore Sun* reported that "76 German-American Societies of Baltimore completed an elaborate ten-day program of entertainment for officers and crew of the cruiser *Emden*." A day later, the paper reported: "Mayor Announces Courtesy Visits Will Be Exchanged With German Officers" (April 17, 1936). Despite growing opposition to the visit, newspaper stories announced that schoolchildren would be taken on tours of the ship, and students at Goucher College were planning a reception for the crew. Then from Washington came the announcement that the *Emden*'s captain would be the guest of Chief of Naval Operations William H. Standley at a Navy Department luncheon.

The *Emden* affair was a bonanza of propaganda for local pro-Hitler German societies. They announced elaborate plans for entertaining the ship's officers and crew. Led by the local German consul, the pro-Nazi societies met with the mayor to receive official blessing for their plans. The press printed an interview with one of the ship's officers who boasted about how many British ships he had sunk in the final days of the First World War when he was a submarine officer.

The League's executive secretary, Sam Swerdloff, had no difficulty assembling a committee of 50 people[23] to express opposition to the German "goodwill" visit. Dr. Edward L. Israel, rabbi of the Har Sinai Congregation, led a delegation that called on Mayor Howard W. Jackson to protest his planned official greeting of the Nazis. The mayor blamed Secretary of State Cordell Hull for arranging the greeting. Public opposition to the events welcoming the German ship continued to grow. Commander Charles S. Houck, Jr. of the local American Legion declared that "at least some of the signers of the protest proclamation lean to the radical and communistic elements of the city," and that it "would be an insult" to the German visitors for the Legion to cancel its part in the welcoming events.

The local Artists Club distributed 50,000 leaflets calling for a demonstration at the waterfront. More than 3500 people marched through Baltimore on April 19, carrying caricatures of Hitler and signs denouncing the Nazis. A League press release stated: "We want to stage an orderly protest but we want to make it plain that despite the official city reception, the people of Baltimore are not welcoming emissaries of the Nazi government." The signs included: "We're With the German People and Against Hitler"; "Congratulations on Destroying Democracy"; "Congratulations on Murdering the Labor Movement"; "Congratulations on Persecuting Minorities"; and "Congratulations on Burning Books." Goucher College students, meanwhile, canceled their planned dance for the Nazi cadets.

The mayor and the American Legion commander finally announced that they were canceling their official reception for the *Emden*'s crew. The entire police force of 2000 was put on a 12-hour-watch to prevent marchers from getting too close to the pier. The *Emden* pulled out of the Baltimore harbor amid reports that similar demonstrations were being planned in several other ports in the U.S. and Canada.[24] The following April, several men dressed in "full Fascist regalia" according to a *Baltimore Sun* editorial (April 5, 1937), attempted to disrupt one of our League neighborhood street meetings. A leaflet distributed by the League shows a photograph of the group dressed in Italian fascist uniforms with blackjacks at their side, giving the Mussolini straight-arm salute to the American flag.

War in Africa Too

When Mussolini invaded Abyssinia (later called Ethiopia) in 1935, the peace movement had a third continent to contend with in addition to Asia and Europe. Mussolini had a decade earlier seized power in Italy in 1922, crushing every independent Italian political and social voice. He now made known his determination to build an empire based on Abyssinia's natural resources.

In a "Proclamation Against War," the American League Against War and Fascism's National Bureau called on ordinary citizens to step in where diplomats had failed to prevent the last independent country in Africa from losing its autonomy. The League was critical of the weak embargo the Roosevelt Administration had ordered on arms sales to Italy. The League urgently recommended stopping the sale of supplies to Italy for making weapons, and demanded the prohibition of loans and credits to the Mussolini government.

The League invited all like-minded organizations to join together to support its actions against Italy. The League also sponsored the formation of a Committee for Ethiopian Independence. More than 50 union leaders of the AFL signed the committee's Proclamation of Labor in support of Ethiopian independence.[25] Delegates to the AFL's 1935 national convention passed a resolution officially adopting the proclamation.

The public campaign in support of Ethiopian independence was launched with a large mass meeting at Madison Square Garden on September 25, 1935, backed by the city's leading labor officials, including George Meany, president of the New York State Federation of Labor. (He was later the founding head of the American Federation of Labor and Congress of Industrial Organizations, the AFL-CIO.) One month later on October 26, 1935, some 50,000 people marched on New York streets urging the U.S. government to impose a strict embargo on Italy. An American Youth Congress committee, of which I was a member, met in November 1935 with Assistant Secretary of State R. Walton Moore. We unsuccessfully sought government imposition of a strict embargo on the sale and shipment of war materials to Mussolini. The first priority of the League's peace program was to "work toward the stopping of the manufacture and transport of munitions and all other materials essential to the conduct of war, through mass demonstrations, picketing and strikes." (*Fight*, February 1936).

Photograph showing labor support in 1936 for the movement against war and fascism at meeting in New York to commemorate Henri Barbusse (photograph in background), French novelist and founder of the World Congress Against War. Speakers left to right included Heywood Broun, founding president of the American Newspaper Guild; Dr. Harry F. Ward, chairman of the American League Against War and Fascism; and John L. Lewis, president, United Mine Workers of America.

Although not widely publicized, protests against shipping war goods to Mussolini for his war against Ethiopia were having some effect. In December 1935, the crew of the ship *Spero* docked in Hoboken, New Jersey, walked off the job when they found it's cargo contained scrap iron bound for Italy. Dock workers in Seattle also refused to load cargo destined for Italy that could be used for military purposes. Despite all protest efforts, Ethiopia remained an Italian colony up to the very end of the Second World War.

Merchants of Death

In one of my diverse roles at the League, I closely followed developments in the armaments industry. The more I learned about the industry, the more aware I became of the manufacture and sale of weapons for private profit. Several international conferences whose goal was to limit international armaments had already fizzled. The conferences were never successful because nations that participated in them continued to contrive in any way they could to get their own special agreements that would authorize them to continue to build weapons.

Those who demanded genuine disarmament, or at least a halt to the burgeoning arms race, were the target of barrages of propaganda paid for by shipbuilders. William B. Shearer, an armaments lobbyist, proclaimed that pacifists, defeatists, "radicals of many hues, foreign agents, communists, socialists, and other organizations with impressive names designed to fool Americans," were giving aid to the enemy. He appeared at a Senate Naval Affairs Committee hearing whose agenda included alleged anti-American activities at the Geneva Peace Conference. (See Chapter Four).

Behind the patriotic slogans of wartime, corporations that knew no national boundaries were operating at hugh profits. This was always their primary motive and they promoted weapons sales to all comers. The German firm Krupp supplied armor plate to all the large navies of the world. British and French arms manufacturers were also active in the hunt for international customers.

The growing public disillusionment with the consequences of the First World War was reflected in an outpouring of books and magazine articles between 1930 and 1934 about the armaments industry, with such titles as *War for Profits, The Secret International, Patriotism, Ltd., Iron, Blood and Profits, and Merchants of Death.* North Dakota Republican Senator Gerald P. Nye undertook a senate hearing on the armaments industry in 1934. Shocking revelations of corruption and greed were forthcoming from subpoenaed corporate and banking witnesses.

DuPont's average annual profit of about $6 million for four previous years soared to over $58 million during the war years, and the value of a share of its stock rose from $20 to $1,000. Addressing a meeting of the Women's International League for Peace and Freedom in Philadelphia, Senator Nye sarcastically referred to the DuPonts as "400 percent patriots. That is the annual profit made by the DuPont corporation during the four years of war." He noted that no other country was spending as much for war preparations as the United States, and charged that "international pacts are easily destroyed or evaded by these munitions makers once they see a chance to make a profit. If we are to have peace," he warned, "profit must be removed not only from war but from preparations for war." (February 9, 1935). Many other industries that contributed to the manufacture of arms experienced similar surges of wartime prosperity.

The purpose of the Nye Committee, officially named the Special Committee on Investigation of the Munitions Industry, was to study the causes of U.S. involvement in the First World War. The findings of the Nye Committee influenced subsequent public support for neutrality and isolationism prior to the Second World War. Information uncovered by the Nye committee also resulted in a nationwide demand for nationalization of the manufacture of weapons as a way to reduce incentives for war. Such proposals were vigorously rejected by lobbyists for the arms industry. Eugene G. Grace, president of the Bethlehem Steel Corporation and Bethlehem Shipbuilding Corporation, told the 1934 Nye Committee hearings that the chairman's plan for 100 percent taxes on war profits would "cripple industry in a time of war." He argued that private industry should be aided and encouraged in time of war. Questioned on his World

War I financial gains, Grace revealed that in 1917-1918 he had received millions of dollars in bonuses.

For nearly two years, as the Nye Committee dug ever deeper into the secret papers of the U.S. War Department, uncovering trails leading to the Department's corporate associates, the hearings made front-page news. The American League Against War and Fascism closely followed the Nye Committee hearings. It arranged a series of meetings across the country at which Senator Nye addressed large audiences. A meeting in San Francisco was attended by more than 4000 people. The League's position was that nationalizing the arms industry alone would have little effect on preventing war. An article in *Fight* pointed out that although Japan, "the most highly militarized country on earth," had a nationalized munitions industry, this fact did not discourage the Japanese government from waging war against its neighbors. Senator Nye's hearings were eventually squelched by elimination of funds needed to continue them.[26]

The League held a People's Congress for Democracy and Peace in Pittsburgh in November 1937, where 1,400 League delegates gathered representing constituents of approximately four million people. At that event, the League declared its support for nationalization of the manufacture of arms, munitions and implements of war.

While the Nye investigation performed a valuable service by exposing the intimate ties between government and arms manufacturers, it did not lead to any legislation or change in the operations of the "merchants of death." A public opinion poll showed 82 percent of the American people favored a government monopoly of munitions manufacturing. This sentiment was put to the test in 1940 when the U.S. government launched an intensive program supporting the private corporate manufacture of armaments after war broke out in Europe. Proposals that controls be imposed on prices charged by American arms manufacturers were discarded when manufacturers threatened not to cooperate unless they were guaranteed a ten percent profit. Thus three years after the overwhelming majority of the American people appeared to support government control of arms production and the end to profit-making from the international sale of arms, a new binge of profiteering began.

CHAPTER SIX

Student Antiwar Strikes

During the years I worked as the organizer for the Youth Section of the American League Against War and Fascism, I kept in close touch with the rest of the antiwar movement that was growing rapidly in the United States and Europe. On February 10, 1933, the Oxford Union, a debating society, made the historic declaration, "This House in no circumstance will fight for King and Country." Randolph Churchill, son of Conservative Party leader and future Prime Minister Winston Churchill, rushed to Oxford University to demand that the minutes of the debate be expunged from the record. Instead, his intervention was followed by a large antiwar vote of 750 to 136 students in favor of the Pledge. Similar motions were adopted by students at other universities in Britain. The "Oxford Pledge," as it became known, also became a major rallying call for students in the United States.

In New York and other U.S. cities, a strike against war was held on April 13, 1934, initiated by the League's Youth Section, the National Student League, and the Student League for Industrial Democracy. About 25,000 students, mainly attending New York City colleges, stayed away from classes on that day. At Brooklyn College, approximately 4000 of the total student body of 5000 left their classrooms and marched to nearby colleges where other student groups joined them. Striking students also came out that day at Columbia, Yale, Harvard, Johns Hopkins, and Los Angeles Junior College. Some college and high school authorities tried to break the movement by punishing participants, using expulsions and other penalties.[27]

American Youth Congress

The economic depression that hit the country in 1929 motivated millions, young and old, to join organizations dealing with its catastrophic effects. "Hunger marches" of the unemployed; student protests against militarism; demands for unemployment insurance; and demonstrations of First World War veterans for payment of bonuses promised them at the end of the war — all these were issues that dominated American political life and helped put Franklin D. Roosevelt into the White House in 1932.

I attended a conference on behalf of the Youth Section of the American League Against War and Fascism, with other antiwar youth organizers at New York University in August 1934. The purpose was to establish a national youth organization called the American Youth Congress (AYC). The conference was organized by 22-year-old Viola Ilma who had recently launched a magazine for young people. It advocated for young people to get more involved in solving the country's critical problems.

A World Congress of Women previously held in Chicago in 1933 had voted to send Viola Ilma to an international women's congress that summer in Geneva. While in Geneva, she took trips to France, Spain, and Germany to take a look at the youth movements in those countries. On returning to the United States, she announced that she planned to convene the AYC to establish an organization that would speak for America's young people. She sent me a lengthy portfolio of material about the new organization. The information preordained how it would be run and who would be its leaders. This hardly seemed an example of democratic procedure.[28]

Representatives of twelve organizations already dealing with the effects of the Depression on young people and threats to democracy, such as fascism in Europe, began to meet together informally to examine Ilma's ideas and the undemocratic procedures that she established in advance of the conference. We agreed to attend the congress, but drew up a set of proposed changes to create more democracy in the proceedings.[29]

Ilma and her supporters lost control of the congress at its initial session. They announced that the planned organization would be led by a body consisting of one delegate from each participating organization at the congress, regardless of their size. There would be 20 representatives of "unaffiliated youth," whom she personally would select. She would become permanent chair of the organization. Amid shouts of disapproval from delegates, a young man stood up. This was Waldo McNutt from Topeka Kansas, representing the Rocky Mountain Conference of the YMCA. He made a motion that in the interests of democracy, the delegates themselves elect a chair for the opening session. llma abruptly adjourned the meeting and announced that the congress would reassemble that evening. At the evening session, despite Ilma's efforts to regain control, McNutt was elected chair by a vote of 62-41. At this point, Ilma called on her supporters to follow her to the Brevoort Hotel to hold their own separate congress.

Representatives of youth organizations, including myself, who had met in the weeks preceding this gathering to consider their position on Viola Ilma's proposals to organize an American youth movement, had never heard of Waldo McNutt. We later learned that he had political roots in a radical movement going back to before the First World War in Kansas. Somehow a notice about the conference, addressed to the Rocky Mountain region of the YMCA headquarters in Denver, had found its way to McNutt in Topeka, Kansas. His appearance at the conference and his debating and organizational skills ended up changing the course of the historic New York youth congress.

The day after Ilma left the congress with her followers, the *New York Times* (August 18, 1934) reported that their group had adopted "a much milder platform" than those who remained at New York University. It called for the easing of birth control laws, divorce by mutual consent, and federal support for education. As important as these issues were, they were not what was uppermost in the minds of millions of unemployed youth. The congress that remained at New York University included nearly 2000 delegates who represented more than 1,700,000 young people in 79 different organizations. They placed priority on addressing the needs of the masses of young Americans who were not only dealing with the economic effects of the Depression but were now facing growing international militarism and fascism.

The delegates adopted the name American Youth Congress originally proposed by Ilma, and announced plans for regional congresses across the country. We elected a Continuations Committee of 15 people to plan future activities. Among the committee's members were representatives of the Student Christian Movement, the National Student League, the Young Communist League, International Ladies Garment Shipping Clerks Union, the National Student Federation of America, National Municipal League, Young People's Socialist League, Young Negro Cooperative League, and the Industrial Council YWCA. Ilma had inadvertently become the catalyst for what would develop into the most effective and broad-based youth movement of the time.[30]

The program adopted by the delegates at New York University in August 1934, cited the fact that six to seven million young people under the age of 25 were jobless, many having never experienced the opportunity for employment. The program further called for specific measures to prevent what appeared at that time to be the impending militarization of youth through creation of the Civilian Conservation Corps (CCC) and military training in high schools. The AYC also condemned racially segregated schools, supported trade unions for young people, and proposed expanded educational opportunities.

AYC continued to gain wide acceptance among students, farm youth, religious organizations, and the new industrial union movement. Unlike the American League Against War and Fascism, AYC did not attempt to enroll individuals but instead functioned only through its affiliated organizations. The successful program that had emerged at New York University in August 1934 came about largely by improvisation. The second congress, held the weekend of July 4, 1935, in Detroit, would reveal that AYC was firmly established.

After an extensive League organizing trip through the Midwest in spring 1935, I set out for Detroit to help set up the upcoming AYC congress. We were preparing for 1300 people representing 846 organizations from 26 states. This meant finding meeting facilities and a hotel to house all the delegates. Under pressure from the local Hearst newspaper who accused AYC of being under communist control, several hotels turned us away before the Fort Wayne Hotel finally agreed to accept our business.

Determined that there would be no barring of black delegates, we insisted that the hotel sign a contract guaranteeing not to discriminate. However, the guarantee vanished with the arrival of the first black delegates. Only our threat to withdraw all the delegates, which would leave the hotel virtually vacant over the July 4th weekend, forced the management to back down. All but six of the twenty restaurants with prior nondiscrimination agreements with us reneged on those agreements. During a large welcoming party for delegates, a line of 600 pickets formed in front of the Fort Wayne Hotel when its drugstore began charging black delegates double for drinks and ice cream in direct violation of Michigan law. After the local police threatened to use tear gas, the proprietor of the drugstore decided to close for the night and the picketers went back to the party.[31]

We next had to deal with the local school district, which illegally denied us access to a school facility for our sessions. We took the ban to court, where Judge Frank Toms ordered district officials to open Cass Technical High School for our use. A small but noisy group of about 75 people, including former Republican Governor Wilber M. Bruckner, chairman of the American Legion's Americanization Committee, tried unsuccessfully to block our entrance to the school.

At the Detroit congress, delegates adopted a Declaration of Rights of American Youth:

> ... on this Fourth of July 1935, we, the Young People of America, in Congress assembled ... announce our own declaration of Rights. We declare that our generation is rightfully entitled to a useful, creative, and happy life that guarantees full educational opportunities, steady employment at adequate wages, security in time of need, civil rights and peace.

The declaration proceeded to spell out a program to achieve its goals. One of its unprecedented undertakings was to draft national legislation called the *American Youth Act* for passage by the U.S. Congress. It would create jobs and vocational training, establish a system of unemployment and social insurance, minimum wage and shorter hours, as well as educational opportunities for everyone between the ages of 16 and 21, without discrimination.[32] The Senate Committee on Education and Labor eventually held two sets of extensive hearings on the bill in March of 1936.[33]

Waldo McNutt decided, after being reelected AYC chairman at the Detroit meetings in 1935, to leave the AYC and concentrate on building the American League Against War and Fascism. He was succeeded as AYC chair by William Hinckley, a psychology teacher and native of Yankton, South Dakota. Meanwhile, Joseph Cadden, a graduate of Brown University who had been secretary of the National Student Federation, the coordinating body of college student governing organizations, was elected AYC executive secretary. He held this position for most of the organization's existence. An effective and unflappable organizer and administrator, Cadden had the ability to reach out to diverse organizations making up the AYC constituency. The organization continued to thrive under his leadership.

As the peace movement grew, the student program became even more specific in its demands. It called for creation of college courses in peace education and passage of the *Nye-Kvale Bill* in Congress, which would make high school and college military training optional. It fostered legislation that would prohibit loans, credits, and war materials to the Italian government. This was a direct response to Italy's invasion of Abyssinia, now Ethiopia. (*Fight*, November 1935).

After the third AYC congress in Cleveland, I set out by train for Toronto to talk to youth members of the Canadian League Against War and Fascism about developments at the Cleveland meetings. As the train crossed the border from Buffalo, an inspector asked me why I was going to Canada. I was worried that if I mentioned "antiwar" I might be turned back, so I replied "sightseeing." This led him to ask how much money I had. He then took out a pad and wrote out an "Order for Deportation," citing as reason, "Sec. 3. 55 J, Insufficient Funds." At the first Canadian border stop, I was ordered off the train and directed to take the next train back to the States.

The movement against militarism and war continued to expand. There was a circulated appeal for a mobilization for peace to take place on November 11, 1935, to mark Armistice Day, the anniversary of the end of the First World War.[34] On November 11, an estimated half million of the nation's students stayed away from classrooms. Following that action, a delegation representing the organizations that sponsored the national strike the year before, plus students representing several college antiwar groups, went to the White House at the invitation of President Roosevelt. We foresaw this as an opportunity to present our views in Washington. However, rather than holding the expected discussion of the war, the President launched into an exposition of his "good neighbor" policy toward Latin America. We were then ushered out of the office. At least I was able to report in my *Fight* column (December 1935), that this was the first time the President had officially recognized the existence of the student antiwar movement.

Poster from student peace strike at the University of California, Berkeley, April 1935. Courtesy of Bancroft Library, University of California, Berkeley

ALLSTON WAY

Photograph of student antiwar strike at Sather Gate, University of California, Berkeley, April 1936. Four thousand students left classes to join the protest, and local labor unions took part in the demonstration. Courtesy of Bancroft Library, University of California, Berkeley.

A month later in December 1935, student delegates gathered in Columbus, Ohio, at a historic meeting to merge the socialist-led Student League for Industrial Democracy and the communist-led National Student League into the American Student Union (ASU). Thus another major student organization established a national presence in addition to the AYC. The delegates declared that the new organization "accepts without reservation the Oxford Pledge to refuse to support any war conducted by the United States government." Through the ASU, students began advocating for abolition of the ROTC, took up the cause of the Spanish Republic, and supported Chinese students defending their country against Japanese invasion.

On April 22, 1937, a Christian-oriented group, the United Student Peace Committee, organized another national student strike. This effort brought about an uneasy alliance between Christian groups, many of them pacifist, and groups that had wider political and social agendas. These differences were a replay of similar difficulties that had faced the American League Against War and Fascism throughout its existence. The National Intercollegiate Christian Council resolved that it was possible "to cooperate with an organization of a different nature on points of mutual interest without giving an O. K. to everything the organization stands for...." The resolution stated that the world situation was so serious that cooperation was much more important than the differences among the student groups. ("*On the Campus*" by Helen Morton, executive secretary of the National Student Council of the YWCA, in *Fight*, April 1937).[35]

League of Nations

In 1936, the same year the American League Against War and Fascism had held its third congress in Milwaukee and the American Youth Congress met for its third congress in Cleveland, the International Federation of League of Nations Societies held a World Youth Congress in Geneva to bring together young people from around the world. Although the United States had never joined the League of Nations, the AYC welcomed an invitation from the U.S. branch of the Federation of League of

Nations Societies, a nongovernmental organization, to attend the meeting in Switzerland.

More than 700 delegates from 35 countries, including representatives of ten international youth organizations, assembled in Geneva during the week of August 31-September 7, 1936. There were 38 elected delegates and 14 observers from the U.S. All international delegates met in the *Batiment Electoral*, the building where the League of Nations Assembly regularly held its sessions.

American delegation to First World Youth Congress on board ship to Europe, August 1936. Jim Lerner standing at railing, right.

For the first time since the 1917 Russian revolution, Soviet youth participated in an international gathering that cut across ideological lines. Among the international organizations that sent delegates were the International Federation of University Women, the Young Men's and Women's Christian Associations, the World Student Christian Federation, and the Young Communist International. Even the international Boy Scouts sent an observer. At first, some of us worried about whether fascist delegations from Germany, Italy, and Japan would show up, as these had been invited in accordance with the League of Nations principle of universality. But when none showed up, the mood of the Americans quickly changed from one of relief to one of disappointment that we wouldn't have the chance to directly challenge them.[36]

A report on the Geneva proceedings issued by the British Youth Assembly, *The World We Mean to Make*, noted that the Americans created a great impression "when at the Inaugural session they sent a colored delegate to speak on behalf of the American continent." That delegate was Edward Strong, representing the National Negro Congress.

Unlike the delegations that were selected as if they were government deputations, the Americans were only accountable to the peace groups we represented. We jointly determined that our role was to actively press other groups at the conference to openly take positions against fascism and make themselves visible as advocates for world peace.

The American delegates wondered among themselves whether the youth of smaller countries that were getting pressure from Hitler to join a "new world order" would speak out for peace. First the Czechoslovakian delegation, and more surprisingly, delegates from Bulgaria, Poland, Romania, Denmark, Belgium and Switzerland, all took forthright positions. They openly expressed fear over growing threats from the fascist countries and advocated collective security against them. A year before, almost to the day (September 14, 1935), in the very League of Nations Assembly hall in which we were meeting, Soviet Foreign Commissar Maxim Litvinoff denounced the refusal by leading Western nations to act against Germany and other aggressor nations. He warned that "peace is indivisible;" that war once tolerated in some parts of the world would spread to others. This phrase "peace is indivisible" became an international rallying cry to oppose the rise of fascism.

Two young people from China and Spain whose countries were in the eye of the storm made a deep impression on the delegates. Loh Tsei, a young woman in traditional Chinese dress spoke of the Japanese invasion of her country's northeastern provinces, in violation of existing peace treaties and the League of Nations Covenant. She had been arrested with other Chinese protestors for denouncing the government's focus on anticommunism while a Japanese invasion was taking place in the north of the country.

After he personally witnessed the arrest of Loh Tsei and other students at Tsing Hwa University on December 16, 1935, the American correspondent Edgar Snow (*Red Star Over China* and *The Other Side of the River*) cabled the story to the United States and Great Britain. It was in this way that the Chinese students' activities against the Japanese invasion came to the attention of the Paris-based International Student Union. As a result, the arrested Chinese students were invited to participate in the World Youth Congress in Geneva that September and Loh Tsei was chosen to be a delegate. The Chinese students' struggle against the Japanese invasion thereafter became part of the mainstream world youth movement against fascism.[37]

I had already heard about Loh Tsei even before the Geneva World Youth Congress. Several months before coming to Geneva, the League received a report about the arrest of the Chinese student leaders. The Youth Section of the League circulated a petition among American student leaders protesting the arrests in China and forwarded it to Chinese authorities. In the September 1936 issue of *Fight*, just before the Geneva congress, the League reported receiving a letter from the Chinese students thanking us for our support. Now, here in person at the convention, was Loh Tsei herself. She and I became friends there and continued a lifelong correspondence.[38]

A Spanish delegate at the Geneva Congress, Gustavo Salgado, one of a group of 18 young Spaniards, described the critical situation in their country. Only six weeks earlier, the fascist leader General Francisco Franco had launched a rebellion against the democratically elected government of Spain.[39] Another delegate, Alfonso Garcia Robles from Mexico, challenged the American delegation to show where they stood on the Monroe Doctrine and its support for Latin American dictators. This "doctrine" had been unilaterally declared by the United States more than 100 years earlier, in 1823. It held that the American continents were "henceforth not to be considered as subjects for future colonization by any European Power." The purpose of the Monroe Doctrine was to establish U.S. hegemony over Latin America, and it led to a number of military interventions and support for Latin American dictators. After Robles spoke, I got up on behalf of the American delegation and condemned the use of the Monroe Doctrine as U.S. policy toward Latin America. I reassured everyone gathered there that young people in the United States would continue to fully support democratic movements in Latin America.

Each country's youth delegation selected the subjects that they would present to one of the three commissions into which the congress was divided. The American delegates chose "collective security," as opposed to the isolationism prevalent in the U.S. at that time. This position was contrary to the position of many socialists and pacifists who supported isolationism because they felt that there was no way for capitalist governments to adopt a viable peace program.

Participants at World Youth Congress, Geneva, Switzerland, September 1936.

I reported back to the larger assembly in Geneva, on behalf of our group, that the American people did not have much confidence in the League of Nations because of its manifest failure to stop aggression in Europe. Nevertheless, I observed that the isolationist attitude that had prevailed in our country since the end of the First World War was gradually diminishing and Americans were now taking a renewed interest in world affairs. I also reported that most of the American youth represented by our delegation favored collective security.

A number of delegations, including ours, were determined that deeds must follow the idealistic speeches and resolutions of this unprecedented international gathering. We pressed for follow-up actions to convince governments around the world that young people were resolutely committed to resisting any threats to peace. American Student Union Chairman Joseph P. Lash proposed that November 11, the anniversary of the First World War Armistice, be used for international demonstrations in favor of disarmament. Plans for this worldwide event would include a second World Youth Congress to be held in the United States, a Pan-American Youth Congress where young people from countries that were victims of the Monroe Doctrine could have a forum for their views, and an impartial delegation to Spain that would report back on the fascist threat to democracy in that country.

CHAPTER SEVEN

Staying the Course

The right of black and white delegates to stay in the same hotels and eat in the same restaurants had to be fought for again and again wherever we tried to convene AYC meetings. In Cleveland, a year after the hotel confrontations in Detroit, despite all our advance preparations, we had to find substitute meeting facilities for the AYC congress the night before the opening session. There just was not enough time to negotiate with several hotels over the issue without canceling the entire congress.

Now in June 1937, Joseph Cadden and myself arrived in Milwaukee early in the month to prepare for nearly 200 expected delegates to the fourth AYC congress to be held in early July. Once in Milwaukee, we made the unfortunate discovery that the local Aerie of the Fraternal Order of Eagles operated the hall contracted by AYC. We found out that the hall, plus several hotels we planned to use, intended to refuse accommodations to all black participants.

During the following few weeks leading up to the conference, hardly a day passed without an article about the Eagles' discriminatory actions appearing in the local press. This included the largest daily newspaper, t*he Milwaukee Journal, and the Milwaukee Leader*, the city's socialist newspaper. The *Leader* (June 17, 1937), reported that the NAACP and the National Urban League were among the organizations sending delegates to the youth congress. In all, about 200 of the 2000 delegates expected were black. When we sought intervention by Walter P. Mattison, the Milwaukee city attorney, he responded by saying that anyone could "use his own property to bar niggers if he wants to."

Prominent local citizens joined the protests and a *Leader* editorial declared:

> On June 18, 1937, the front page of the *Leader* reported that Robert W. Hansen, vice president of the Milwaukee Aerie, away on legislative duties in Madison, wired his objection to the ban on black delegates. He reminded the hall manager that the motto of the Fraternal Order of Eagles is "liberty, truth, justice and equality."

Despite the statement from one of its principal officers about equality, and the editorial, the hall was never made available to AYC.

While Cadden retained a former assistant city attorney, William F. Quick, for possible legal action, I left for Madison to confer with Wisconsin's attorney general, Orland S. Loomis. He declined to take any action on the grounds that the Eagles Club was "privately owned and operated" and it was therefore under the jurisdiction of the local Milwaukee courts (*Milwaukee Journal*, June 20, 1937.) On that same day, the press reported that two-thirds of the city's hotels had refused to rent rooms to delegates attending a convention of the organization called the Workers Alliance, a major national organization of the unemployed. Although these events later led to the introduction of a bill in the Wisconsin state legislature raising penalties for discrimination, they did not help solve our immediate need for accommodations.

We could not wait any further for legal action to give us access to a hall for the conference, so we accepted the offer by the Brotherhood of Locomotive Engineers to use the large Milwaukee municipal auditorium for our open public meeting. At the time, the engineers were renting the hall for their own convention. Meanwhile, the major hotels had shut their doors against us and only the threat of lawsuits, backed by public outrage, convinced several other hotels to finally accept our delegates. While we had to cope with the inconvenience of meeting in three different halls (the Auditorium, the Pabst Theater, and the fifth floor of the Schroeder Hotel, which had initially barred our black delegates), at least the AYC had made a lasting contribution to democracy in Wisconsin through major anti-discrimination rulings that came out of our actions at the Milwaukee congress.

The Milwaukee congress turned out to have the largest number of participants compared to any prior national gathering of American youth. Farm, labor, religious, student, women, socialist, communist, peace, and Girl Scout officials were among those who gave their support, as did 11 United States senators and 33 members of the House of Representatives. In preparation for the congress, AYC produced a 36-page illustrated publication called *Youth.* It described, with pictures and comments, how the Depression affected young people. This was the only time I solicited a commercial advertisement, a full page spread by the Milwaukee Brewers' Association, titled "A Salute To Youth."[40]

Delegates at the Milwaukee congress were divided into a house of representatives and senate, modeled on the U.S. Congress. There were a number of committees, including agriculture, labor, civil rights, education, and recreation. We formed one committee the U.S. Congress lacked, a peace committee. Members of the AYC national board served as a cabinet. At the World Youth Congress in Geneva the previous August, the U.S. delegation had promised to develop a relationship with Latin American youth as one of its major goals. As part of this commitment, three representatives from Cuba attended the Milwaukee meetings.[41]

The NBC and CBS networks broadcast the deliberations of the congress. While concerns at the congress over unemployment and threats to world peace attracted major public attention, issues of crime, education, and health were also on the agenda. National and local experts spoke at all sessions. [42]

In the middle of all the difficulties we were encountering, a newspaper story provided our committee with a bit of comic relief. *The Wisconsin News* (June 21, 1937) reported: "Trouble dogs the path of the Model Congress of Youth meeting here in national convention July 2-5. Whether free beer shall be served and whether the 2,000 delegates shall visit Milwaukee's famous breweries are the latest problem." The story quoted Joseph Cadden and myself as opposing the free beer offer because of expected delegates from 40 Protestant denominations and the Women's Christian Temperance Union.

Arrests at German Embassy

The following year, delegates to the next AYC national congress in Washington D.C. in March 1938, were jolted out of their discussions on jobs and education by news that Hitler had occupied Austria. The Germans had arrested Austria's president and confiscated Jewish businesses. The press reported that hospitals were beginning to expel Jews from their positions, and all Aryans were ordered to wear armbands with swastikas. Those of us at the Washington conference were well aware that the Austrian path to fascism had already been laid four years earlier, when the socialist, communist, and trade union movements were crushed by violence and arrests.

The national office of the now-named American League for Peace and Democracy (formerly American League Against War and Fascism) supported my idea of organizing a protest demonstration in Washington D.C. at the German embassy. Thirty of us from AYC and members of the Fur Workers and National Maritime Workers unions picketed the embassy on March 13, 1938. A law enacted by Congress only a month before had prohibited such activity within 500 feet of a foreign mission or embassy. We carried improvised signs with such slogans as "Treaty Breakers Are War Makers," "Boycott Nazi Germany," and "Down with the Swastika." Our band of protesters broke up into smaller groups and marched from several different directions toward a fenced-in hill. We wanted to make it more difficult for the police to corral us while we approached the embassy. When Hitler's ambassador Hans Heinrich Diekhoff drove through the embassy gate in his big blue limousine, we began shouting, "Keep Hitler's bloody hands off Austria." Within minutes, the police arrived and herded us into a group where we waited for patrol wagons, called "Black Marias." Another group of picketers arrived as we sang the national anthem. They too were arrested.

The police who had grabbed signs out of our hands began shoving us into the police wagons. We loudly sang peace songs and shouted anti-Hitler slogans, as we were driven through the capital to the city jail. The notorious head of the Washington "red squad" ordered us to be finger-printed and photographed. The demonstration and arrests made front-page news in Washington and elsewhere.

Arrested antifascist demonstrators singing protest songs inside paddy wagon at German Embassy in Washington, DC, in 1938, after Hitler's invasion of Austria. Jim Lerner at far left, facing camera.

Ours was the first defiance of the law prohibiting picketing within five hundred feet of a foreign mission. The press, which we had alerted to our plans, reported the demonstration as a constitutional test of the law. *The Washington Times* carried a two-column photograph of the demonstration and a long story headed, "Groups Held For Marching at Legations" with a subheading, "Counsel To Be Hired For Test of Law." At the bottom of the page, a seven-line item reported that Franco's forces had swept within 30 miles of the border of Catalonia in Spain (March 14, 1938).

Two weeks after the demonstration, eight of our group were sentenced to 30 days in jail. They pleaded guilty and their fines were paid by the

ACLU. Trials for myself and a young member of the National Maritime Union were set for a later date as part of an ACLU plan to test the law's constitutionality.

The appearance of newspaper stories about a demonstration by fewer than thirty young people was just an initial sign of growing attention and anger in America at the crushing of an independent nation by Germany. Yet the invasion of Austria merely served as a prelude to world war. The "bloodless" conquest of Czechoslovakia by Germany followed several months later.

Although I had initially come to Washington for a weekend meeting, I was now out on bail and faced an indefinite stay. The demonstrators who were waiting for the first trial needed food and lodging and had to be kept busy to keep from becoming demoralized. We also needed to raise funds in Washington and in New York City to meet the expenses of our arrests. We sent small delegations to meet with some liberal members of Congress at the House Office Building. Some of the female members of our group reported they were having to fend off aggressive sexual approaches from congressmen and their staff. A well-known member of the House offered $50 to one of the young women who came to see him if she would agree to return after office hours. After that, I sent a male member of our group with each female to any congressional visit.

In a report describing the first trial, *The Washington Post* wrote that the district attorney frequently repeated the words "red-blooded Americanism" and questioned the patriotism of anyone who opposed the anti-picketing law. He claimed that members of the ACLU "are attempting to hide behind the Constitution that — by their own unlawful and unconstitutional acts — they are attempting to tear down." The next day the *Washington Herald* reported that Colonel Julius Peyser "was severely criticized by indignant members of the National Defense Through Patriotic Education Committee of the Daughters of the American Revolution for defending the protesters." Thus, opposition to a Nazi invasion had become an attack on "Americanism." Numerous youth organizations protested against the arrests and convictions as did at least six members of the

House of Representatives and one senator, Gerald Nye of North Dakota, well-known for his investigation of corruption in the munitions industry.

Eventually, the Supreme Court refused to accept our appeal, thus keeping the embassy picketing law on the books. The law continued to be enforced for nearly 50 more years to intimidate and punish picketers, including hundreds of people arrested at the South African embassy in Washington D.C. in 1985. In 1987, the Supreme Court finally declared the law unconstitutional.

End of the Youth Movement

At the last AYC congress held in New York City during the first week of July, 1939, representatives gathered from 736 member organizations. Attempts to yet again divert the AYC meeting into a debate over communism failed. *Time Magazine* reported that 16 New York City councilmen and 56 state legislators had expressed their support for an anti-communist resolution at the conference. However, delegates resented such outside interference and proceeded to overwhelmingly defeat the resolution. *Time* also reported that one of the supporters of the anti-communist resolution jumped up and shouted "all patriots follow me." The report went on to say that "out of the hall marched 11 of the 1,450 delegates and observers" (*Time*, July 17, 1939). The AYC congress unanimously adopted a resolution that placed the organization on record as opposed to "all forms of dictatorship, regardless of whether they be Communist, Fascist, Nazi or any other type." The resolution further reinforced AYC's longstanding intention to keep its organization open to supporters of all political views.

Eleanor Roosevelt, who continued to openly support the AYC, attended the first day's session and wrote of her impressions in her nationally-syndicated newspaper column on July 6, 1939:

> I was tremendously impressed yesterday to read the resolution passed by the American Youth Congress. The effort which has been made to brand the congress as Communist-controlled and the final effort which was made to stampede them into doing something which would have been completely undemocratic, has been, I think, wisely handled. On

> the whole, the leadership of the congress seems to me to be very sane. It may be a little idealistic, but then if we can't have ideals in our youth, what will happen to us when we are old?

Following this final 1939 AYC congress, several thousand young people went to Washington D.C. for the organization's National Citizenship Institute held on February 9-12, 1940. During a drenching rain, a large group of students marched through city streets to the White House lawn where AYC Chairman Jack McMichael reported that more than four million American "young citizens" were still out of work. In an address from the portico of the White House, President Roosevelt assured the crowd that they had the right to hold any political views they wanted. But some boos arose from the group when he then criticized those in the student movement who were refusing to condemn the invasion of Finland by the Soviet Union in November 1939. This incident was widely reported in the press.

The National Citizenship Institute held its meetings at the U.S. Labor Department auditorium where the rain-soaked crowd had marched after seeing the President. At these sessions, the AYC chairman criticized liberals and progressives in government for failing to achieve passage of the *American Youth Act* that AYC had worked so hard to see enacted into law. Following speeches by delegates and invited experts, Eleanor Roosevelt remained in the audience and spent a solid hour patiently responding to a barrage of questions. She brought up the Soviet invasion of Finland as President Roosevelt had done earlier at the White House. This was an issue that was deeply fragmenting the American peace movement.

Professor Robert Cohen has described how the CYA's confrontation with President Roosevelt brought to a head the issue of "dual loyalty" that existed within the CYA leadership. On one hand stood their commitment to the broader student movement and on the other hand, to the Communist Party.

> It was, in fact, because communists had served the student movement so faithfully prior to the Nazi-Soviet Pact that their behavior after the Pact came as such a shock to many non-communists in the movement.

> After years of unity and cooperation with communism, it was difficult to believe that they would sabotage a student movement that they had been so instrumental in creating.... Blinded by their loyalty to the Soviet Union, the communists failed to see the disastrous consequences of forcing the movement's key organizations to defend a Soviet deal with Hitler and invasion of Finland that most students found indefensible. (*When the Old Left Was Young*, Oxford, 1993, pages 305-306).

Cohen further shows how those on the American political right took advantage of the break-up of the once powerful student movement. "Seizing the moment, conservatives along with some liberal anti-communists, launched a series of legislative red probes, loyalty oath campaigns, and moves to restrict free speech rights...." (*When the Old Left Was Young*, page 307).

AYC never recovered from the splits in the organization caused by the August 23, 1939 *Non-aggression Pact* between the Soviet Union and Germany, and the Soviet Union's subsequent invasion of Finland. However, in its seven years of active existence between 1933 and 1940, it helped keep together a broad coalition of youth organizations which, at its peak, had a national membership of more than 4,700,000 people. Its members had reason to believe that they had helped bring about the progressive legislation of the New Deal. They had also directed the anger and frustration of America's youth away from the kind of right wing movements that brought fascism to power in Europe. The next great youth movement would not arise again until the antiwar movement of the 1960s.

CHAPTER EIGHT

Brink of World War

Brussels

As the World Youth Congress was winding up its deliberations in Geneva in early September 1936, another major international gathering, the World Peace Congress, had been convening in Brussels, Belgium. Originally scheduled to be held in Switzerland, this meeting had to be moved because of the antagonistic atmosphere created by the Swiss press against grass roots peace movements.

Lord Robert Cecil, the chairman of the League of Nations Union in Great Britain, and Pierre Cot of France were the principal organizers of the 1936 Brussels congress. Two separate American delegations, reflecting the major divisions within the American peace movement, went to Brussels. One was headed by Dr. Harry F. Ward of the American League Against War and Fascism, and the other by John Nevin Sayre of the National Peace Council. On the eve of the meeting, the two American groups agreed to unite at least as far as the Brussels sessions were concerned by approving the joint chairmanship of Ward and Sayre. This was an encouraging development to those who had long hoped for a more unified American peace movement.

As the price of being allowed to meet in Brussels, the Belgian Minister of the Interior required that the congress not raise "political" issues or mention the war in Spain. Even the word fascism was a taboo. Despite the prohibitions, members of a Spanish delegation, on the way to France to seek support from the French Popular Front government headed by Socialist Premier

Leon Blum, were greeted with enthusiasm at the congress. American League delegate Margaret Forsyth reported (*Fight*, November 1936) that although the Spanish antifascist leader *La Pasionaria* stood silently before the assembly, the expression on her face amply showed a story of courage and faith.

It took extreme discipline for the 4,000 delegates to follow the many restrictions. Delegates in cafes, corridors of hotels and meeting rooms could be heard discussing how the restrictions made it difficult for the congress to accomplish anything. After several days spent ensuring that the congress would not totally come apart, the delegates agreed on an International Peace Campaign based on a four-point program: 1) promote international agreements to reduce and limit armaments; 2) strengthen the League of Nations; 3) prevent and stop war by more effective organization of collective security (this became known as the controversial "sanctions plank"); 4) recognize the sanctity of treaty obligations.

To support this program, delegates agreed to set up a loose federation of member countries. An international team of speakers would go from country to country to promote the peace campaign. Despite the limited program adopted by the delegates, the League felt that an important step had been taken toward building a unified international antiwar movement.

It was not long before efforts in the United States and Canada to promote the Brussels peace program ran into problems. Enthusiasm for the principle of "collective security" faded as the idea crossed the Atlantic. We also found on returning home that the excitement that had stirred delegates in Brussels, where all shades of political opinion joined together to support one program, was not shared by everyone in the traditional American peace organizations.

The National Peace Conference, a clearinghouse for 34 peace organizations in the United States (not including the American League Against War and Fascism), chose not to participate in the International Peace Campaign initiated by the Brussels meetings. They objected to the inclusion of communists in the campaign and to the sanctions that would be imposed on countries who did not support the four-point program. While the League pushed ahead to promote the International Peace Campaign, there continued to be only a meager response from other American peace organizations.

The Fellowship of Reconciliation opposed the Brussels peace campaign because of the sanctions plank. The National Council for Prevention of War was opposed because of communist participation and emphasis on collective security. Six months later, Winston Churchill and other prominent British leaders officially signed a document endorsing the doctrine of collective security. Even this historic event did not arouse any new enthusiasm for collective security within the United States peace movement.

Progress was also slow in accomplishing one of the first goals of the new movement, the planning of national peace conferences. Even scheduling internationally known speakers for lecture tours was so tenuous that by fall 1937, the International Committee that had been formed in Brussels decided not to send anyone from abroad to speak in the United States. Acceptances for membership in the National Committee of the International Peace Campaign had come from only ten organizations, all of them small groups, except the League and the Young Women's Christian Association. The Canadian League Against War and Fascism was running into similar difficulties.

Still hanging on, the shrinking American committee of the International Peace Campaign wrote to President Roosevelt and the State Department on May 24, 1937. The letter stated that since Italy and Germany had openly acknowledged their participation in the war to overthrow the Spanish Republican government, the United States should now apply its arms embargo policy against them. The State Department replied, "This department has received no evidence which would in any way warrant the belief that arms exported from the United States subsequent to the enactment of the Joint Resolution of January 8 [1937] have reached Spain." The outbreak of the Second World War was only two years away when our efforts to build a broader, more inclusive American peace movement foundered.

Second World Youth Conference at Vassar

In 1938, the same year the American Youth Congress met in Washington D.C., a second World Youth Congress took place in August at Vassar

College in New York State. In contrast to the First World Youth Congress that the International Organization of the League of Nations sponsored two years earlier in Geneva, this one was initiated by international youth groups themselves with AYC as host. [43]

As they arrived on huge ocean liners at New York harbor, international delegates were treated to a spectacular greeting of the type usually reserved for celebrities and war heroes. Dozens of ferries and tugboats unleashed their sirens and the city's fireboats shot spectacular sprays into the skies. At City Hall, Mayor Fiorello La Guardia received a representative international delegation and gave them keys to the city. The mayor addressed 25,000 people who came to a welcoming rally at Randall's Island stadium in the middle of the East River. He said that "more will come from this assembly of youth than from the maneuvers in Europe." For the young people from around the world who had organized the congress, including those who were recently freed from jails, and others who feared imminent loss of their countries to fascism, it was a brief time of great hope.

Jim Lerner with badge at Second World Youth Conference at Vassar College, August 1938.

After spending months helping to put together the welcoming rally for the delegates, I was gratified to watch people stream across the East River Bridge and descend into the stadium on a warm starlit evening. As the delegations from 48 countries marched into the stadium behind their national flags, the entire assembly rose to its feet. There was a special reception for the delegations that were made up of refugees. From Austria came refugees from Germany's invasion of their country; from Spain came young people still fighting to save their democracy; and there were representatives from China, whose country was under brutal attack from a Japanese invasion. An opening pageant was put on by a group of American professional performers who were part of the Federal Theatre Project, the program that provided employment in performing arts during the Depression. We were entertained by a chorus that sang American spirituals and folk dancers from many of the countries that were represented at the multinational gathering.

Assistant Secretary of State A. A. Berle represented the United States government; Joseph Cadden greeted audience and delegates on behalf of AYC; Elizabeth Shields-Collins of Great Britain spoke for the International Continuations Committee set up at the Geneva Congress; and Ernest Kalibaler spoke on behalf of the peoples of Africa. At the previous 1936 congress in Geneva, only whites attended as representatives for Africa.

During sessions held in the following days, Eleanor Roosevelt sat through the meetings, often doing her knitting. She wore earphones, to hear the translation of the many languages spoken by delegates. She had also attended many meetings of the National Council of the American Youth Congress over the years. In meetings with us and in her daily newspaper column "*My Day*," Roosevelt often expressed her political and social views. She had once described her trip to a town where several despairing unemployed workers had hanged themselves. She criticized those who "sit in comfortable offices and write editorials for great metropolitan newspapers and ... say that we should not have relief that tries to provide the kind of work people can do."

Eleanor Roosevelt, with translation headphones, knitting at Second World Youth Conference at Vassar, August 1938.

While there had been not a single representative of labor unions in the American delegation at the previous First World Youth Conference in Geneva, here at Vassar there were several affiliates from the new Congress of Industrial Organizations (CIO), including UE. In addition to labor representatives at the Vassar meeting, the presence of observers from a number of government agencies reflected AYC's stature at that time.

For the U.S. delegates, the presence of a large contingent from Latin American countries was especially significant. At Geneva, there had been a single Cuban, Carlos March, then living in exile in the United States. Now there were 36 Cubans representing labor unions, agricultural workers, and university students. From Mexico, where the single delegate who came to Geneva challenged the Americans on their attitude toward the use of the Monroe Doctrine as an instrument for dominating Latin countries, there were now 50 official delegates and approximately a dozen observers. The delegates spoke for workers, students, artists, teachers, and writers. Evidence of Latin American interest in the Youth Congress was seen also in the unanimous vote of endorsement for its delegation by the Chilean parliament. The president of Argentina himself served as head of the sponsoring committee for his country's delegation.

Thirty-six young people came from China, including Loh Tsei, who had made an impressive presentation at the youth conference in Geneva when she spoke about the invasion of her country by Japan. Twenty-two delegates from Czechoslovakia brought heightened attention to the fact that Hitler was poised to invade their country. Delegates from Ethiopia, India, Indonesia, British West Indies, the African Gold Coast, Korea, and Uganda brought home the reality of colonialism in large areas of the world. The colorful international dress of delegates from all over the world lit up the Vassar campus.

At the youth congress in Geneva two years earlier, delegates were subject to many restrictions regarding the conduct of meetings and which countries were allowed to attend or speak. In comparison, the atmosphere at Vassar was open and exuberant. Enthusiastic ovations greeted delegates from Spain, China, Czechoslovakia, and Austria, whose countries were already in the forefront of the world's struggle against tyranny. Americans fighting in Spain with the Abraham Lincoln Brigade sent greetings.

Resolutions called for an embargo on the supply of war materials to Japan, boycotts of Japanese goods, and the lifting of embargoes on the sale of arms to the Spanish Republic. Delegates expressed strong opposition to any recognition of Italian sovereignty over Ethiopia and urged Great

Britain and other nations to join in the collective defense of Czechoslovakia. The congress approved a six-article "Peace Pact" that pledged delegates to work for unity with young people of all countries in the quest for peace and social justice.

One of my happier memories of the Vassar congress was the boat excursion taken by delegates from a number of countries down the Hudson River. It was a bright, sunny day and we did a lot of singing, in many languages. Some delegates waved flags of their countries. The wide Hudson and its surrounding hills shimmered in the background.

The mood became more somber as delegates prepared to return to their countries. On the ship back across the Atlantic, the French delegation learned of the agreement at Munich, between Hitler and the heads of the British and French governments that surrendered Czechoslovakia to Germany in the name of preserving peace. "The return home was sadder than the voyage out," the writer Simone Tery wrote in *Danielle, The Wonderful Story of Danielle Casanova* (published originally in France and then in the United States in 1953). Tery reported that French delegates to the World Youth Congress who were on board were often ashamed to look at the Czechoslovakian delegates returning on the same ship.

In the spring after the Vassar congress, Hitler's armies overran France. In the face of great personal danger, Danielle Casanova wrote and distributed publications and organized demonstrations for the French underground that called for resistance to fascism. The Nazis eventually seized and tortured her. Danielle was among 230 women crammed into cattle cars and shipped off to the Auschwitz concentration camp in Poland where she died of typhus. Of this group, fewer than 50 women lived to return after the war.

Within a year of the Vassar meeting, many delegates from European countries found themselves up against guns, bombs, concentration camps, or exile. Michael Wallace, treasurer for the Geneva Congress, died fighting as a member of the British air force. The secretary of the Austrian Committee for the Second World Youth Congress didn't make it to Vassar because he was thrown into a concentration camp shortly before we were to convene. Erich Jungman, a German student who came to the Vassar conference from exile in Paris, was seized and disappeared into a concentration camp when Hitler invaded France.

Within a year of the Vassar meetings, the fascists under Franco defeated the Spanish republic. Other countries in Europe and Asia fell one after another to the German fascists and their Japanese allies. What happened to many other young people who had come from Poland, Belgium, and other places where the Nazis spread their terror? Those of us who got to know them on the peaceful Vassar campus in 1938 never knew.

CHAPTER NINE

A General's Warning

Fear of Fascism in America

A harsh antidemocratic and antiunion national climate cast a shadow over the League's third congress in Cleveland in January 1936. General Motors was just one of many large corporations that formed special committees to fight union organizing. Other companies included General Electric, Goodyear, Westinghouse, Standard Oil of New Jersey, American Telephone and Telegraph, DuPont, U.S. Steel, and International Harvester (*Labor's Untold Story* by Richard Boyer and Herbert Morais, 1955). One of the most respected "captains of industry" in 1936 was David Sarnoff, head of RCA, who engaged the well-known gangster, Sam Cohen, to help break a bitter but eventually successful strike led by UE at the company's Camden, New Jersey, plant. The National Association of Manufacturers launched a nationwide campaign against unions, summed up in the title of their booklet, *Join the CIO and Help Build A Soviet America.*

Michigan served as the base for Father Charles E. Coughlin, a Catholic priest, who ran a national radio program heard weekly by millions. He published a nationally distributed publication, *Social Justice* that promoted an American version of fascism. Beneath the title "The Peacemakers," Coughlin wrote an article praising Hitler and Mussolini in which he said that unlike communism, fascism allowed free elections and "freedom of political action." (*Social Justice*, October 3, 1938). Father Coughlin's followers held meetings in halls and at busy intersections in the New York City boroughs of Brooklyn and Queens. They sometimes incited their converts to enter nearby subway stations and attack Jews.

One of our League members wrote to the national organization: "We have been confronted by a distressing situation in the Flatbush and Kings Highway sections of Brooklyn.... Under the guise of Catholicism ... a group has been active for six or seven months preaching anti-Semitism and intolerance." Many in the Catholic Church, outraged by Coughlin's activities, spoke out against him. Cardinal Mundelein of Chicago made clear that the Michigan priest did not speak for the Catholic Church. Meanwhile, League members distributed to Protestant and Catholic churches our pamphlet about the League's coalition with church organizations. We sometimes faced open hostility. Eventually, Father Coughlin was silenced by the Catholic Church.

It was part of the League's program to expose and organize against anti-democratic groups, which included the American Legion. Supposedly nonpolitical and nonpartisan, the American Legion had since its founding after World War I promoted legislation conflicting with the Bill of Rights. It had been used to break strikes and labor unions, had interfered with free speech and freedom of assembly, and had been a vociferous opponent of peace organizations.

A decade before the American League Against War and Fascism was organized to help alert the American people to the dangers of fascism, Alvin Owsley, a National Commander of the American Legion, laid out the Legion's possible future role as protector of the country's "institutions and ideals." He praised the fascist government in Italy for dealing with "obstructionists," and stated that the American Legion was prepared to assist the American government to do the same. Recognizing kindred spirits among its leaders, Benito Mussolini annually sent greetings to the American Legion's national conventions. William Edward Easterwood, Jr., a national vice commander of the American Legion visited Mussolini in 1933 to confer on him an honorary membership.

In many towns and smaller cities, there were American Legion posts made up of working people and poor farmers who saw the local Legion hall as a place for socializing, having a beer and organizing an occasional party. It was to such war veterans that the American League Against War and Fascism appealed to urge resistance to the national commanders who honored fascists and promoted violence in the name of fighting subversion. At the 1935 American Legion convention in Pennsylvania, Governor George Howard Earle expressed his disagreement with the Legion's pro-fascist position. He warned delegates that America was in great danger "if we heed the deceptive cries of special privilege, if we permit our men of great wealth to send us on a wild goose chase after so-called radicals...."

As the antifascist and labor movements grew and began to challenge corporate power, organizations such as the Ku Klux Klan resurfaced. New ones with such names as Silver Shirts, Sentinels of the Republ*ic, Khaki Shirts, Black Legion, Black Shirts, Brown Shirts, and Christian Front*[44] harassed and intimidated those who were expressing themselves on issues of democracy and peace. Ridiculous as such organizations may sometimes have seemed, dressed up in uniforms mimicking Mussolini's Blackshirts and Hitler's Brownshirts, the violence they used in breaking up peaceful gatherings became very destructive. It was significant that Michigan was the center of such fascist sympathy because workers there were trying to build an industrial union in the powerful automotive industry.

Because of the increasingly hostile antidemocratic environment developing in the country in the mid 1930s, it became an important goal at the 1936 League congress to persuade the American people to recognize the characteristics of fascism. These included the restriction of civil liberties, the promotion of racism, and the suppression of workers' rights to organize. In hindsight, fear that fascism of the type that occurred in Europe would take over in the United States were not borne out. However, the damage to American civil society caused by racism and the constant obstruction put in the way of organizing efforts for union rights and social justice was so great that it can still not be measured today.

CLEVELAND

In January 1936, more than 2000 delegates from 30 states, Puerto Rico, and the District of Columbia came to Cleveland for the third congress of the National League Against War and Fascism. Seventeen pre-congress conferences were held around the country to prepare for the Cleveland meeting. Commissions on trade unions, women, farmers, youth, education, national and racial minorities, veterans, religion, literature and war and fascism made proposals for action. Each commission brought in experts in the field. The education commission was chaired by LeRoy Bowman, Director of the United Parents Association in New York City and a member of the League's national board. The commission heard Robert Spivack, editor of the University of Cincinnati college newspaper, tell of the pressures being put on high school and college students to join the ROTC.

Professor Dorothy Douglas of Northampton, Massachusetts, spoke about the close connection between teacher oath requirements passed in 22 states, antilabor legislation, and the denial of civil rights. Among this commission's recommendations was for the League to encourage "a campaign for the removal of anti-labor, anti-Negro, pro-war and pro-fascist propaganda" from school textbooks.

The mayor of Cleveland, Harold Burton, came to greet the delegates on behalf of the city, despite demands by some League opponents that he steer clear of the congress because of alleged communist influence. Veteran labor leader Max S. Hayes welcomed the congress on behalf of the Cleveland Federation of Labor. Arrows that were placed on the city's lampposts pointed the way to the Public Auditorium for the opening public session. Signs about the meeting were posted in street cars, making several thousand delegates from all over the country feel welcome.

Poet Langston Hughes addressed some 10,000 people at the opening public meeting on the subject "The Negro Faces Fascism." He pointed out that physical intimidation and violence, long suffered by black people, was now increasingly being experienced by other groups.

> Poor white workers have been set upon by mobs; labor organizers have been run out of town, tarred and feathered and even lynched; people whose ideals have not been in agreement with the powers that be have been denied due process of law and have suffered legal discrimination...." (*Proceedings, Third U.S. Congress Against War and Fascism*).

In speeches across the country, Hughes criticized the ongoing United States military buildup: "Has America any real fear of invasion from abroad?.... Is not the answer rather that we have colonies and world markets to maintain which provide profits for a select few?" (*The Life of Langston Hughes* by Arnold Rampersad, 1986).

Methodist Episcopal Bishop Edgar F. Blake of Detroit also addressed the opening rally, and warned that "Chambers of Commerce, Manufacturers' Associations, Liberty Leaguers and their subsidized satellites" were attempting to suppress the rights established in the Bill of Rights." Other speakers included Rabbi Barnett R. Brickner of Cleveland, Wyndham Mortimer, a founder of the UAW, and retired Marine Corps major general, Smedley Butler. [45]

At the League's congress in Cleveland, an international session took place with speakers from Canada, Cuba, Brazil, Mexico, Germany, and China. An anonymous message was read from Japanese Christians living in the United States expressing opposition to their country's war on China.

Undoubtedly the most unusual speaker at the Cleveland congress was General Butler. He described how he came to understand the repressive role the U.S. government had played in Latin America during his many decades of military service. His widely-publicized statement to a Congressional committee in 1934 on the role of American forces in Latin America served as a powerful confirmation of the ideas long held by those of us who opposed U.S. intervention:

> I spent thirty-three years and four months in active service as a member of our country's most agile military force — the Marine Corps. I served in all the commissioned ranks from second lieutenant to major general. And during that period I spent most of my time being a high class muscle man for Big Business, for Wall Street, and for the bankers. In short, I was a racketeer for capitalism. Thus I helped make Mexico and especially Tampico safe for the American oil interests in 1914. I helped make Haiti and Cuba a decent place for the National City Bank to collect revenues. I helped purify Nicaragua for the international banking house of Brown Brothers in 1909-1912. I brought light to the Dominican Republic for American sugar interests in 1916. I helped make Honduras "right" for the American fruit companies in 1903. In China in 1927, I helped to see to it that Standard Oil went its way unmolested.

As he sat on the platform at the Cleveland congress, General Butler's red, rugged face and prominent hooked nose contrasted with the faces of union leaders, clergy and professors seated alongside him. These men had established their reputations speaking and writing, sometimes at great peril to their standing in the community, against the very military and government activities to which Butler had devoted most of his life. Pounding the lectern as he spoke in a hoarse, rasping voice, the General exclaimed, "War is a racket.... It is conducted for the benefit of a very few at the expense of the very many." In a fervent plea for American neutrality in the war that he saw coming, he urged League members not to "permit our flag to be prostituted by being used as a protecting blanket to cover gun-running or to protect the interests of a few manufacturers or international bankers."

Following the Cleveland congress, the League sponsored a national tour for General Butler, including a symposium in San Francisco on April 22, 1936. A leaflet advertising the meeting identified the general as "Champion Orator Against War" and "the only living military officer who has been awarded two Congressional medals of honor." It went on to say that Butler was a "keen student of military strategy, a skillful leader of men, and author of the sensational expose, *War Is A Racket*" (1935, Round Table Press.)

I once went to Butler's home in a Philadelphia suburb to ask him to write about his military experiences for publication by the League. He came striding down a wide central stairway that was flanked by military banners representing the battles he had led. In his new role, Butler was now confirming the peace movement's conviction that behind the noble words of the Monroe Doctrine were imperialist designs by American bankers and their corporate allies. It was difficult to tell what moved Butler to switch sides. It certainly wasn't money, because the small fees paid by organizations such as our American League were a pittance, if anything; nor was it prestige, because he was addressing meetings of a peace organization that throughout its existence battled charges of being communist-dominated. Let it be said that his conscience triumphed.

During the sessions that followed the opening ceremonies, those conducted by the 350 youth delegates grew at times by twice as many people because of older delegates showing up. They came into our sessions attracted by dynamic events happening at that time in the youth movement, especially national student antiwar strikes.

Youth delegates at the congress, originating from a wide scope of philosophies, including Christian youth groups, passed a number of resolutions. These included criticism of newspaper and magazine publisher William Randolph Hearst for his opposition to government measures for easing the country's economic depression. And despite their antipathy towards communist ideology, some Christian groups adopted resolutions calling for freedom for Angelo Herndon, a young black communist who faced 22 years on a Georgia chain gang for organizing the unemployed. They also demanded the release of nine boys from Scottsboro, Alabama, who were facing the death penalty on a rape charge that was generally regarded as false. At the time, the Communist Party was making major national issues of both cases.

One outcome of the third congress was a resolution to broaden the League's outreach. Robert Morss Lovett, League vice-chairman, who was professor of English at the University of Chicago and president of the League for Industrial Democracy, announced that official representatives of the Socialist Party were ready to support a resolution to create a joint committee with the League. He stated that this "would bring together a more inclusive federation of antifascist and antiwar forces." Paul Porter of the National Executive Committee of the Socialist Party, who was present at the congress as an observer, assured delegates that "the Socialist Party is willing to give full support to the resolution entered here. We have no reason to doubt the good feelings or mutual trust of any individuals or groups participating in the American League." Earl Browder of the Communist Party also supported the resolution, thereby temporarily raising hopes for a broader expansion of the League's membership. However, the Socialist Party's expression of trust notwithstanding, the Party leadership continued its longstanding refusal to become an official part of the League.

Charles Zimmerman, who was at the congress as an official observer for the International Ladies' Garment Workers Union, also supported the resolution to expand the League. He reported that while the executive board of his union recognized the accomplishments of the League, a broader trade union base was needed to make the movement against war more effective.

The passage of the resolution to expand the base of the League brought "great applause and ringing cheers" from the delegates, as recorded in the convention report. However, later efforts by the League to obtain broader support fell short of its goal. The garment workers' union failed to join the League. We later learned that the garment workers actually favored the dissolution of the League altogether and promoted the founding of a new organization as the way to achieve broader unity. However, the replacement of a functioning organization by one not yet in existence never won support among the League's ranks.

Changing Direction

The American League Against War and Fascism's fourth Congress in Pittsburgh took place on November 26-28, 1937. The 1,416 delegates who attended represented organizations with more than 4,000,000 total members. This was a sharp increase over the Cleveland congress in 1936, especially in trade union representation. There were 413 labor delegates who spoke for 1,600,000 trade unionists, a nearly three-fold growth over the previous year. This increase reflected the League's growing ties with the burgeoning industrial union movement.

The League assigned me to assist the Pittsburgh branch in setting up the 1937 Congress. I approached hotels and restaurants for reservations and I also contacted owners of meeting facilities to find a place big enough for several thousand people to gather for the opening public session. Once again, racism showed up as a major obstacle to making conference arrangements. After meeting with officials at several hotels, I wrote Gert:

> The William Penn, one of the major hotels, has offered me an office and lodging free of charge for the duration of my stay in the city — about two months — if I would sign an agreement not to send them Negro delegates. When I indignantly rejected this outrageous proposal, they suggested a "verbal understanding" to the same effect, which I also turned

down. On top of this attempt to enforce "apartheid," our arrangements committee has learned that the management of the hall we had rented, and for which we had already put down a $200 deposit, had changed its mind about renting to us.

The absence of halls that could seat the large number of people we expected became critical. And it was not only a matter of barring black people. We also discovered that the national head of the Americanism Committee of the American Legion, Homer Chaillaux, pressured the owners of the hall to reject us because the head of the Communist Party, Earl Browder, had ties to the League. Fortunately, some of our members who were active in Pittsburgh politics were able to persuade leading politicians, including the head of the local Republican Party, to intervene on our behalf. We finally secured a large hall, the Duquesne Gardens, and I began ordering tickets and posters.

We were unable, on the other hand, to get the major hotels in Pittsburgh to provide rooms to our delegates regardless of their color. Threatened with legal action, one hotel manager told me "to hell with the law." We finally managed with great effort to obtain rooms for most of the 1,416 delegates. At the opening session of the Congress, delegates voted to demand equal treatment for all and agreed that if the barrier against equal treatment for whites and blacks could not be broken, the white delegates would leave the uncooperative hotels and support a civil rights lawsuit against them. Four black delegates had already started a lawsuit after being turned away from a hotel. Picket lines of several hundred conference delegates marched at the entrances to the hotels who had refused to accommodate the black delegates.

Under an eight-column headline across the top of page one, "Race Delegates Barred," *The Pittsburgh Courier*, one of the country's major black newspapers (December 4, 1937), reported: "The greatest bombshell ever exploded against discrimination practices by the management of downtown Pittsburgh hotels and restaurants was hurled Saturday by New York delegates attending the People's Congress for Democracy and Peace [sic] held at the Motor Square Gardens in East Liberty." The newspaper described legal actions and appeals to the mayor and governor initiated by the League. The paper also reported that some white delegates persuaded hotel desk clerks to let them register for late-arriving friends. When the friends turned out to be black, the management at major hotels, including The William Penn, refused to honor the registrations. The Courier reported:

> Outside [the hotel] 300 delegates marched ... shouting "Equal Rights for every race." Grant Street traffic was jammed by motorists who stopped to witness the picket line. They heard one of the pickets, Morris Schappes, a white delegate from the American Federation of Teachers and instructor at the City College of New York, who had mounted a parked car in front of the hotel, shout to the growing mass of cars and pedestrians: "The management of the William Penn has forbidden me the right to sleep and eat in the same building with my colored brothers and sisters. Something has to be done to break the back of the monster called discrimination."

White delegates withdrew from the William Penn while a picket line of over 300 delegates walked in front of the hotel to make the public aware of the hotel's practices.[46]

The number of people entering the spacious Duquesne Gardens in Pittsburgh for the opening public session of the fourth congress was estimated at 5000 by the press. Several pickets shouted "communists!" and carried signs identifying themselves as members of a local Catholic Radical Alliance headed by the Reverend Charles Owen Rice. Acknowledging in a statement to the press that "many sincere and praiseworthy progressives and labor leaders have been and are mixed up in this League," the priest said that this was only because they have been "duped" by communists. He pleaded with union members "not to cooperate with the communists." In contrast, Congressman Jerry J. O'Connell (D-Montana) told the opening meeting, "I am a Catholic, I bow in no way in my Catholicism to any man or woman on that picket line, and I say to them that there is nothing in my religion that tells me I can't fight against fascism and war."

The presence of a large group of trade unionists at the congress had a decisive impact. Trade unions were interested not only in the League's concern with issues of war and peace, but also its steadfast commitment to defend the right of working people to organize as a fundamental tenet of democracy.[47]

As at the three previous League congresses, speakers from many different nations told of the difficulties they faced as defenders of peace and democracy. American delegates reported to the congress that there was growing support in the United States for the Republican forces in Spain, for the League-sponsored consumer boycott campaign of Japanese goods, and for actions on the East Coast to stop the shipment of war goods to Italy.

Two months before the League's 1937 congress convened in Pittsburgh, President Roosevelt expressed his support for an international quarantine of aggressor nations as a means of preserving peace. Encouraged by what appeared to be a departure from the government's "neutrality" position, Chairman Ward outlined a program at the conference based on the principle of "quarantining the aggressor."

The delegates cheered Representative John T. Bernard (Farmer-Labor Party, Minnesota) when he announced his intention to introduce in Congress an amendment to the Neutrality Act of 1937. The proposed amendment would "clearly and sharply distinguish between aggressors and the victims of aggression." The expected effect would be to restore to the Spanish republic and to China their capability of buying arms in the United States.

Several months later, Secretary of State Cordell Hull informed embargo opponents that he would not advise the President to withdraw enforcement of the Neutrality Act against Spain because to do so would threaten the peace of the United States. Hull also stymied efforts to hold a hearing on congressional legislation that would have required withholding economic aid to aggressor nations. So strict was continued enforcement of the embargo against Spain that Mexico had to guarantee that no arms, munitions, or implements of war sold from the U.S. to Mexico would be shipped to Spain. The President's speech on "quarantining the aggressor" thus passed into oblivion.

Reporting on efforts to broaden the League's base of membership and support, Chairman Ward said he had come up against two recurring obstacles: one was the negative name: "Why isn't your organization *for* something instead of *against*?," and secondly, the Communist Party's affiliation with the League. The intent of the League's founders was to have a broad national political representation including the Socialist Party, but it became increasingly evident at the Pittsburgh congress that getting already-established national organizations to affiliate with the League was no longer a viable prospect.

The Socialist Party had on repeated occasions failed to officially join the League. We had not won formal support from major labor unions even when their leaders and many members approved of the League's purpose and actions, and even when they sent delegates to conferences and national congresses. Various peace organizations, including some that were represented at the League's founding, also failed to formally become affiliates. The War Resisters League had a policy to take an uncompromising stand against all wars and would not join any group that was not completely pacifist. The fourth League congress at Pittsburgh, with the support of Earl Browder, Communist Party general secretary, finally voted to exclude all national political organizations, including the Socialist and Communist Parties, from formal affiliation with the League. Another major change came at the congress when the name "American League Against War and Fascism" was changed to "American League for Peace and Democracy."

The League thus made a historic shift from its initial intent to be comprised of national organizations, to a broader-based, more grass roots orientation. The Pittsburgh congress adopted a plan, with the support of union leaders, to set up special committees within local labor organizations to promote membership in the League. Assisted by a trade union organizer from the League, more than 160 local unions in the New York City area cooperated with the League by selling *Fight* and by acquainting their members with the League's goals. A common theme was "Keep the United States out of war and help keep the war out of the world."

I was tired of being away from home so much and had been urging the League's national officers to find a replacement. They asked for some additional time and persuaded me to stay on in Pittsburgh to help the local chapter continue to build its membership. During Christmas week, 1937, I wrote home:

> The weekend has cost me all of 35¢. I had ten dinner invitations during the week but used only five. Last night I moved into my fourth home in two weeks. I've had fine beds but that isn't sufficient for sleep and I keep awake for hours trying to get you out of my mind.

In early 1938, I returned home to New York and resigned my position with the League after being Youth Organizer for seven years. After that, I continued to be a member of the League and helped organize conferences and programs as a volunteer.

Cover of the June 1937 issue of Fight Against War and Fascism, *published monthly between 1933 and 1938. The woodcut by artist Louis Lozowick refers to the feature story on labor in the courts.*

CHAPTER TEN

War Front in Spain

On our way to Geneva on August 25, 1936, the American delegation attended a meeting in Paris of about 80,000 people in support of the Spanish republic. The Front Populaire, anti-fascist coalition that had energized the democratic forces of France, organized the huge gathering held at the stadium Velodrome Buffalo. The noted writer Andre Chanson chaired the meeting.[48] Signs all around the stadium proclaimed "*Des Avions pour l'Espagne*" (airplanes for Spain). Workers from entire factories marched in support of their pledge to help purchase airplanes for Spain. One of the airplanes stood on the field.

The stadium rocked with shouts of approval at the announcement that workers at the Citroen auto plant had voted to donate one hour's wages a week for planes to Spain. Many in the crowd wept along with Maria Luisa de Labra, a young woman from Barcelona, as she pleaded for armaments and airplanes from French factories.

When we were in Geneva at the youth conference, six Americans[49] joined by four delegates from Canada and Cuba, accepted an invitation from the Spanish delegation to visit their country. After returning to Paris from Geneva, we boarded a train for the French Mediterranean coast city of Cerbere. A representative of the Spanish People's Front met us and told us that all rail service between the neighboring countries was suspended because of the war.

Laden with baggage. we proceeded on foot into a dark railroad tunnel cut into the foothills of the Pyrenees. Behind us, we could see the terraced sides of the hills overflowing with masses of ripening grapes. Our guide's flashlight was our only light as we stepped precariously from tie to tie in the long tunnel until we finally emerged covered with soot. The sun was shining on the Catalonian town of Port Bou, where a locomotive sat bearing three large white letters on its nose, UHP. In the Catalonian language these letters stood for "Unite Proletarian Brothers." Because the train taking us to Barcelona carried militiamen going to the front, we received enthusiastic greetings at every station along the way. Although Barcelona had not yet been enveloped in actual fighting, evidence of defense preparations was everywhere. When we arrived in Barcelona, the notes of a brass band boomed above the last engine gasps and a large banner greeted us with "Welcome International Delegation."

Barcelona was still behind battle lines, so it wasn't until the second night of our stay that we saw some of the immediate effects of fascist terror. We went to the opera house to see the great cellist Pablo Casals perform and conduct a large orchestra in honor of the Republican fighters. From our balcony seats, we looked down onto an auditorium crowded with wounded fighters. They entered wearing bandages and hobbling on crutches and canes.

Our presence in Spain was widely known. An office at the Barcelona railway station was marked: "Foreign Comrades Coming to Help Spain." Passersby greeted us everywhere we went. A young black man rushed up and asked whether we were the American delegation. He had come from Harlem to fight the battle for Spanish democracy alongside antifascist refugees from Italy and Germany and other countries. He described for us in detail the military situation in the surrounding area.

Our ten delegates from the Geneva Congress were assigned three cars for a 400 hundred mile drive through the province of Catalonia, then on to Valencia and Madrid. We stopped frequently to talk to people about the war. While many Catholic clergy sided with the Republic, the church hierarchy itself openly sided with the fascists. We drove by many piles of rubble, the remains of religious institutions. Local residents told us many churches had been destroyed because they were being used as centers for pro-Franco operations. Meanwhile, in the United States, the Catholic hierarchy openly opposed the Republic and supported aid to Franco.

We were routinely stopped at road intersections to show our passes to guards. We noticed one of our drivers take a cartridge out of his automatic weapon and give it to one of the guards at a barricade. He explained that although all the guards along the road were supposed to be armed, they often had no ammunition. This was similar to other experiences we had throughout our trip. Franco, with his well-prepared conspiracy, had seized most of the weapons held by the country's military forces. The fascists were also getting modern weapons from Hitler and Mussolini who were using the war in Spain as a proving ground for their arsenals. At one defense point outside Madrid, I photographed two teenage boys who were taking turns using the single rifle they shared. They were dressed in overalls and old sweaters. Several thousand men had been waiting days for weapons so they could join the battle.

As we looked down to the valley below where the historic Alcazar fortress stood, we learned that five hundred women and children, all families of soldiers loyal to the republic, were trapped there between battle lines. They were being held hostage by the fascists to ward off an attack by government forces.

On Madrid's outskirts, teenage boys and girls crouching in crude dugouts were appealing over loudspeakers to those on the other side to cross over. Occasionally some did. The crudeness of the operation and the shortage of weapons made it difficult to fully comprehend that the fate of a democratically elected republic was being decided. It was clear that more than a civil war was being fought here and that events in Spain were going to have international repercussions. What we were seeing in those early months of the war was the beginnings of what would become a three-year battle. All too few in Western Europe and in America understood that a fascist victory in Spain was leading to world war.

Volunteers and arms were arriving from other parts of the world to assist the Republican army. The young man from Harlem who we met on our arrival in Barcelona would soon be followed by more than 3,300 more American volunteers of the Abraham Lincoln Brigade. As time was to show, private and unofficial help to the Republic could not match the assistance that Germany and Italy gave to Franco. We were in Madrid when three German planes were shot down over the city. Members of the Republican militia showed us new German revolvers they had captured. And yet American newspapers continued to describe the battle in Spain as a conflict between two opposing Spanish sides with no international complicity.

We left for home after ten days in Spain, deeply moved by the courage of the Republic's defenders. Our determination to do something was reinforced by an experience in Barcelona the day before we crossed the border to France. One of our guides informed us that Dolores Ibárruri, the communist leader known everywhere at home and abroad as *La Pasionaria*, would like to meet with us. In a Barcelona hotel room, we were greeted by a tall, imposing woman with deep, dark eyes. Her long black dress added to the solemnity of the meeting. She had just arrived from Paris, where she had pleaded with Leon Blum, the French Popular Front's Socialist premier, to permit the Republic of Spain to buy arms in France. Blum told her he couldn't take the chance. He said there were fascists also gaining power in France and he didn't want to break with French neutrality. Essentially, France was taking the same position as England and the United States. Four years later in 1940, after Germany invaded Spain, Czechoslovakia, and Poland, Hitler's armies overran France.

Leaving Spain, we retraced our steps through the tunnel. At the French border we encountered hostility from border guards. Apparently motivated by their government's neutrality, they confiscated the posters given to me by Spanish youth organizations. Despite my protests, they refused to return the posters. I pleaded with them to at least let them be sent back over the border to Spain. I never knew what became of them. Shortly after we left Spain, we heard that the fascist army was about to lay siege to Madrid.

When the two black members of our delegation, Ed Strong and Elizabeth Scott, attempted to book passage back to the U.S. on the British liner *Berengari*, they were told by Cunard Line officials that they would not be permitted to travel on the same boat with the rest of us because some white passengers had objected to having them on board. This was the only time in our three weeks of travel together that we ran into such open racism. We had earlier traveled to Paris without incident on Cunard's *Aquitania*, where Ed and I shared a room. When we were faced with the refusal by Cunard to let Ed and Elizabeth sail with us, our group of travelers, together with other delegates from 18 countries who were in Paris following the World Youth Congress, protested vigorously to Cunard officials. This forced them to back down, and we sailed home together as planned.

Neutrality

Back in America, the American League Against War and Fascism continued to raise funds for the Spanish Republic and actively campaigned to lift the international "neutrality" embargo on the right of the Republic to buy arms. A large part of our efforts went through the North American Committee to Aid Spanish Democracy and its youth section, which the League had helped set up. At a Madison Square Garden meeting on October 26, 1936, more than twenty thousand filled the huge hall to hear Marcelino Domingo, president of the Radical Socialist Republican Party of Spain; Isabel de Palencio, Spain's minister to Sweden; and the Reverend Luis Sarasola, a Catholic historian and theologian.

Sarasola insisted that the war in his country was not between "Christian civilization and communism." Americans had been constantly hearing about this either/or dichotomy from the Catholic church hierarchy. Sarasola clearly described the conflict as the result of the collusion between Catholic Church conservatives and fascists to suppress the just demands of Spanish workers and peasants.

In December 1936, I joined a delegation of young people from Spain at the start of a U.S. tour of 65 cities. At the request of the sponsoring committee, we arranged for transportation between stops, accommodations, and publicity. Included in the Spanish group were Josefina Ramirez, a member of the executive committee of the Youth Federation of the Republican Unity Party; Ygnaz Eugenie Imaz, director of the Catholic newspaper *Cruz y Raya*; and Luis Simarro of the Unified Socialist League.

We joined the group for parts of its tour, then left the delegation at times to carry on organizational work for the League.

At the center of the American nationwide campaign against the Spanish Republic stood a pro-Franco, so-called Spanish Relief Committee, headed by Basil Harris, vice president of the International Mercantile Marine Company (of J. P. Morgan banking interests). The committee included Leon Fraser, president of the First National Bank of New York; Ogden Hammond, former U.S. ambassador to Spain; and Thomas F. Woodlock, editor of the *Wall Street Journal*. In opposition to the assistance given to Franco, there was widespread support for the Spanish Republic as evident in large public meetings, petitions, and demonstrations. The League's Trade Union Committee to Manufacture Clothing for Spain produced and sent to Spain more than 100,000 garments.

Before returning home to prepare for a speaking tour of New England colleges about the civil war in Spain, I joined a National Youth Pilgrimage to Washington to promote passage of the *American Youth Act*. Some 4000 young people marched down Pennsylvania Avenue on Washington's Birthday, 1937, carrying huge scrolls bearing petitions signed by a million people. Students marching in caps and gowns dramatized the inability of young people to complete their education or find work in the fields. A contingent of young farmers carried hoes and rakes. Young workers from the coal fields headed towards the White House in miners' hats. At the end of the march, while the rest of us waited outside, a delegation entered the White House to present a mountain of signed petitions to President Roosevelt.

Despite growing national opposition to a policy that kept the Spanish Republic from buying arms to defend itself, the president in January 1937, signed a congressional resolution that established an embargo against shipments both to the Spanish Republic and to the fascist forces. There was only one dissenting vote in Congress from Representative John T. Bernard, representing the Minnesota Democratic Farmer-Labor Party. The conservative *New York Herald Tribune* wrote that enforcement of the embargo against both sides had the effect of aiding the fascists.

American economic support of Japan in its aggression against China stood in contrast to American "neutrality" toward Spain. The U.S. Department of Commerce reported in May 1937, that Japan had bought huge amounts of raw cotton, copper, and oil, and scrap iron from the United States during a six-month period. Even steel from elevated rail structures being torn down in New York City was reported on its way to Japan to be turned into weapons. It didn't seem to occur to those in government who were enforcing the embargo on the Spanish Republic that there should also be an embargo on Japan. Several organizations were vainly calling for a halt to the sale of war materials to Japan and for Americans to refuse to buy Japanese-made consumer goods. Silk was very important to the Japanese economy at that time, and the United States consumed 85 percent of its silk exports. In protest, students attending a national conference at Vassar peeled off their silk stockings and tossed them into a campus bonfire. This incident was widely reported in the press.

Boycott of Japanese goods, sponsored by American League Against War and Fascism in Pittsburgh, 1937.

On January 28, 1938, in Washington D.C., the League of Women Shoppers held a "Life Without Silk" show at the Wardman Park Theatre. Organized by Maxine Finsterwald (also known as Maxine Wood), it opened with an address by William E. Dodd, former ambassador to Germany, and was directed by Lee Simonson, scenic director of the Theatre Guild headquartered in New York City. Nationally-known designers gave clothing for the show. The publicity around this event encouraged similar shows in other parts of the country. Since the silk boycott gave every woman the opportunity to personally participate in the antiwar movement, it gained wide support.

Branches of the American League for Peace and Democracy gave high priority to publicizing the continued sale of war materials from the United States to Japan and the import of Japanese goods. Picket lines at S. S. Kresge stores (a major chain that later became part of Kmart) resulted in promises from the company not to buy any more goods made in Japan. An official of the Woolworth chain said they would stop ordering toys made in Japan if enough consumer resistance continued. Typical of our appeal to consumers were the signs carried at a Pittsburgh demonstration organized by the League that read: "Silk Stockings in Pittsburgh Mean Death in China." This was all part of an international movement that won the support of many labor and peace organizations in other countries including Canada, Australia, Great Britain, France, and Mexico.

On December 12, 1937, Japanese forces blockading Chinese ports sunk the American river gunboat *Panay.* Two people died and 39 were wounded. The Pittsburgh chapter of the League responded by holding a meeting at Carnegie Music Hall on January 14, 1938, to organize a boycott against Japanese goods. This meeting was endorsed by both the Steel City Industrial Union Council of the CIO and the Central Labor Union of the AFL. Meanwhile, through its China Aid Council, which served as a clearinghouse for information and activities on behalf of the Chinese people, the League organized the first U.S. medical mission to China.

Although the League continued to grow in the North, the Southern part of the United States remained practically untouched. I was asked to assist some Virginians to establish League branches. After arriving in

Norfolk, Virginia, in March 1938, following an overnight boat trip from New York City, the first thing that caught my eye was a sign that said "colored waiting room this way." I was stymied in attempts to rent a hall where people of both races could meet. I asked a prominent churchman whether the white ministers would object to having Negro ministers at a meeting. He said "not at conferences." I took this to mean that once a year they gathered at interracial conferences and the rest of the year practiced Jim Crow. The only progress I made toward finding a meeting space was within the labor movement, where I was usually able to get a union hall.

Signs of change toward more support in Virginia for the peace movement came in the form of invitations for me to address a dinner of the Ladies Garment Workers and to write the Mother's Day editorial for the *Norfolk Labor Journal.* This publication was endorsed by the Central Labor Union of the AFL. In the talk and editorial, I encouraged support for the League's peace parades and meetings in order to influence the U.S. government toward a policy for world peace.

In some ways, my experience in Norfolk was even more encouraging than my experiences in other parts of the country. I discovered this when I was asked to address a luncheon of the Townsmen society, an organization of small businessmen. My condemnation of U.S. trade in war materials with Italy, Germany, and Japan was reported in the *Norfolk Ledger-Dispatch* (May 2, 1937). This was a productive forum, because Norfolk was a major shipping port, and any discussion about whether to export war goods was clearly understood by the local population.

CHAPTER ELEVEN

The Pall Of Munich

Several weeks after I resigned as national youth secretary for the American League for Peace and Democracy, the League's officers called on me to make arrangements for the League's fifth congress set for January 6-8, 1939, in Washington, D.C. The seizure of Austria by Hitler and his occupation of Czechoslovakia, with the tacit approval of France and Great Britain, together with the defeat of the Spanish Republic early in 1939, made it difficult for peace organizations to respond to fast-moving international developments. These devastating events sapped the morale of people who had supported U.S. peace organizations and who felt so hopeful at the League's 1937 congress in Pittsburgh.[50]

In 1939, after nearly two complete terms of Roosevelt's New Deal Administration, the cloud of racial discrimination still hung over Washington. I wrote home several days after arriving in the capital that my survey of hotels showed that not one of them was willing to rent a room or meeting hall to the League. We received a letter from one hotel where we had held a previous committee meeting informing us that they didn't care for our patronage because we had included Negroes at a recent meeting. Black people were still restricted to the antiquated facilities located in the capitol's slums. This type of discrimination was a repetition of the experiences I had encountered organizing previous conferences in Norfolk, Detroit, Milwaukee, Cleveland, and Pittsburgh. Alice Barrows, an employee of the U.S. Office of Education, who headed the League's arrangements committee, took our problem to Harold Ickes, Secretary of the Interior Department. He influenced the management of one hotel and the owners of the Rialto Theatre to rent us their facilities for the opening meeting on January 6, 1939.

Following the Pittsburgh congress a year before, League membership increased from 7,600 to close to 20,000 in 36 states and the District of Columbia. There were 61 new branches. The League's China Aid Council initiated protest activities in 50 cities against the Japanese invasion of China. In cooperation with the North American Committee to Aid Spanish Democracy and other organizations, the council sent doctors and nurses to China. It undertook the maintenance of a hospital and sent three ambulances and medical supplies. The League raised money to support two homes for Spanish orphans and collected funds, clothing, and medical supplies for Spain.

Of the more than 1,250 delegates at the Washington congress, the largest single group came from 388 labor unions. These included 15 international unions representing over 2,000,000 people. Altogether, there were 17 subdivisions of the CIO and the AFL. The second largest group was made up of young people, including those from Baptist, Evangelical, Unitarian, and Congregational organizations. In recognition of the importance of building the peace movement among working people, delegates voted to set up a national labor committee, chaired by A. F. Whitney, president of the Brotherhood of Railway Trainmen, with Jerome Davis, president of the American Federation of Teachers, as vice chairman. This committee included presidents of 14 international unions.

The congress opened with its traditional open public meeting on the subject "Labor and Democratic Rights." This gathering attracted far more than the 2,300 people the hall could hold. Speeches by major union leaders testified to the unprecedented affinity between the labor movement and antiwar organizations. Union speakers included A. F. Whitney and Dr. Jerome Davis; B. F. McLaurin, international organizer for the Brotherhood of Sleeping Car Porters, largest union of black workers at a time when segregation and discrimination still dominated the industry; and James B. Carey, president of UE and secretary-treasurer of the CIO.

In his opening address to delegates, chairman Harry F. Ward again denounced the government's policy of preventing the Spanish Republic from buying weapons while refusing to place a similar embargo on the arms going to Germany and Japan. I remember Ward's chant: "Lift the embargo on Spain; put it on Germany, Japan, and Italy; protect the unemployed." Also hanging heavily over the proceedings of the congress was the agreement between Italy, Germany, France, and Britain on September 29, 1938, at Munich that allowed Hitler to occupy Czechoslovakia. At the signing of the pact with Hitler, Prime Minister Neville Chamberlain of Britain claimed that it guaranteed "peace in our time."[51]

League officers reported to the 1939 Congress that when Scandinavian seamen aboard the *S. S. Titania* refused to leave the port of Baltimore because the ship carried 9000 tons of chemicals for the Franco armed forces, it was the League branch in Baltimore that initiated public support on their behalf. The League produced numerous posters and buttons about Hitler's invasion of Czechoslovakia and the French-British-German pact signed at Munich. Altogether, the League distributed more than a million pieces of leaflets, pamphlets, and other materials during the previous year.

By 1939, divisions within the peace movement were beginning to show, and our January 1939 congress proved to be the last. By that year the ability of the League to hold together was being challenged by strongly held opposing views among its members about U.S. involvement in the war in Europe. But despite the increasing public support for facing the Nazi menace with military expenditures, the League continued to reaffirm its basic position of opposition to increases in armaments. It continued to promote the development of a positive peace program as an alternative to the burgeoning arms markets.[52]

The truth was that the League could not counteract quickly enough all of the world events that were having crushing effects on the League and other organizations that during the 1930s had built coalitions in which communists played an important part. The cohesion of the Communist Party itself was seriously affected, as members who had spent years alerting the country to the dangers of fascism now sought reassurance from Party leaders that they were not now betrayed by the Soviet-German Non-Aggression Pact of August 1939. The pact meant that the

Soviet Union agreed not to come to the aid of Poland or any other country invaded by Germany. In response, there were widely reported resignations from the U.S. Communist Party, some by members who had been prominent in building major youth and peace organizations. Many other party members dropped away, confused and bitter at what they saw as a betrayal of the work against fascism that they had undertaken in the face of great difficulty and personal sacrifice.

Divisions over the *Neutrality Act* were also beginning to deeply divide the peace organizations. The Communist Party initially opposed the *Neutrality Act* passed by the U.S. Congress under which all countries, including Spain, Ethiopia, and China, would be unable to purchase defense equipment in the United States. Now the Party reversed its position and opposed efforts to repeal the *Neutrality Act.* Party members now feared that if U.S. arms became available to other countries, they might end up being used against the Soviet Union.

The final annual antiwar march and demonstration organized by the League took place in New York City on August 26, 1939. However, confusion, doubt, and resentment about the international situation and about the policies of the peace movement were evident. Several thousand fewer people attended this event than the year before. League Chairman Ward wrote In *The Amplifier*, the League's organizational bulletin, that "some peace organizations have gone into reverse. More and more are obviously moving in the direction of war.... Other peace organizations have come to a halt." (November 16, 1939.)

Coalition Unravels

Failure on the part of the League's leaders to take an official position on the Soviet-German pact intensified accusations that it was captive to the Communist Party's unquestioned support of Soviet policy. It had always been a basic Communist Party tenet that, as a socialist country, the Soviet Union would never instigate war against another country. Outside party ranks, others among the original founders of the League, including Harry F. Ward, held similar views. Roger Baldwin, a member of the

League's National Bureau, who was jailed for opposing the First World War, informed the press on October 29, 1939, that he had resigned from the League. He stated that the League could no longer accommodate the Communist Party because of its support of the Soviet Non-Aggression Pact with Germany. Baldwin harshly criticized the continued support by many American communists for the Soviet Union despite the position of other League members who strongly condemned the Soviet-German pact. The League's inability to have a clear policy on the Pact undoubtedly helped open the way to subsequent attacks by many peace organizations and labor unions against the Communist Party's continued participation in the peace movement.

After reading the newspaper story on Baldwin's statements, Chairman Ward of the American League wrote him expressing regret that his long-time close associate had failed to wait until the League could declare its position at a conference scheduled to be held in Philadelphia a few weeks later. In addition to their shared leadership in the League, Ward and Baldwin had served as chairman and executive secretary of the ACLU since its founding in 1920.[53]

While the League and other peace organizations were grappling with the dilemma of what position to take toward the war in Europe, the same debate was taking place in the labor movement. In 1939, CIO President John L. Lewis declared that "organized labor is emphatically opposed to any involvement in the European war" (October 10, 1939). A CIO resolution confirmed this position days later.

Ward reported that he had been receiving a deluge of questions from League members about the Soviet Union's renewal of a trade pact with Germany and its signing of the nonaggression pact. Ward asserted that if in fact it became clear that an act of aggression by the Soviet Union through the "nonaggression" pact was being committed, it was the League's obligation to call for the same type of embargo against the Soviet Union that the League was demanding against Japan, Germany, and Italy. In the apparent hope that developments in Europe might make such a step unnecessary, Ward emphasized that the League's main concern was keeping the United States out of war and protecting democracy at home. For this reason, the

League's monthly magazine *Fight* was renamed *The World* early in 1939. After only three more issues, Dorothy McConnell, the editor, and several other staff members were laid off from lack of funds. [54]

Despite almost universal hatred of the Nazis, there was such widespread concern that the United States might be drawn into the war that President Roosevelt sought to reassure the country that he had no such action in mind. On October 27, 1939, the *New York Times* reported that Roosevelt had reaffirmed neutrality, and said that, "Boys of American Mothers won't go abroad."

In addition to condemnation of the Soviet Union for its pact with Hitler, anti-Soviet sentiment swept the country following the Soviet invasion of Finland in November 1939. After failing to persuade the Finnish government to trade some of its territory bordering Leningrad for Soviet border territory elsewhere (in order, it claimed, to establish a more defensible zone for its second largest city), the Red Army entered Finland. These events further weakened the League's ability to survive.

Although the League had in effect ceased to be a functioning organization, in its bulletin (November 16, 1939), the League's officers continued to propose that the U.S. stay out of involvement in the war. However, within two weeks, on December 2, 1939, the League's officers found that they could no longer maintain that position and issued another statement in which they urged that all war supplies, loans, and credits be withheld from the Soviet Union. By this time it was all a meaningless effort.

It wasn't until June 22, 1941, when the Nazis, in defiance of the Soviet-German Non-Aggression Pact invaded the Soviet Union, that there was a turnaround in the U.S. Communist Party's stand toward the war. They went from a "hands-off" policy favoring neutrality to one of full support for defeat of the fascists. The British government, now led by Prime Minister Winston Churchill, immediately welcomed an alliance with the Soviet Union. The United States joined the alliance after the Japanese attack on Pearl Harbor in Hawaii on December 7, 1941. The American Peace Mobilization now ceased to exist.

The bitterness aroused by the Soviet-German pact among those who worked unwaveringly to avoid war was felt long after the eventual Allied victory over Hitler. Looking back at the Soviet-German pact after the war, Sumner Welles, assistant secretary of state in the Roosevelt Administration, admitted (*Time for Decision*, p. 322) that the Munich Agreement in 1938 had confirmed to the Soviet government its belief that Britain, France, and Italy were trying to divert Germany toward an attack on the east toward the Soviet Union for the purpose of keeping Hitler from invading Western Europe. For those in the peace movement, there was little satisfaction that came out of learning that many historians and politicians eventually recognized that the Soviet Union had been put in an untenable position by the signers at Munich.

The year 1939 marked the end of one of the most momentous periods in American history. Preparations for war now replaced the years of social advances that began in 1933 under the Roosevelt Administration. I was ineligible for the draft because of the effects of childhood polio. However, many League members and leaders, including Joseph Cadden and former student leader Joseph Lash served in the armed forces.

As for me, I had worked as either youth organizer or volunteer for the American League Against War and Fascism (and under its renaming as the American League for Peace and Democracy) from the time of its first Congress in 1933 in New York until it dissolved in 1939. I now looked back on a decade totally dedicated to working for peace with the hope that our efforts would some day be seen as a lasting legacy for future world peace.

CHAPTER TWELVE

Peace Is Un-American

On August 21, 1938, I read in the newspapers that J. B. Matthews, the former chairman of the American League Against War and Fascism, appeared before the House Un-American Activities (HUAC) as a "friendly witness." Representative Martin Dies of Texas, chairman of HUAC, focused his anti-communist campaign at that time on our American League for Peace and Democracy, the American Youth Congress, and the World Youth Congress. It was no coincidence that the week of August 16-23, 1938, was chosen by HUAC to produce Matthews as a witness. At that time, more than six hundred representatives of youth organizations in fifty-four countries were meeting at Vassar College for the Second World Youth Congress. (See Chapter Eight).

In the years that followed, Matthews provided HUAC with the names of countless men and women, including many government employees connected at one time or other with religious, political, and social organizations concerned with peace and social justice. Some undoubtedly had even been inspired by the "old Matthews" to join the movements he previously promoted and now condemned. League members across the country would for years be harassed and victimized by the McCarthy rampage against democracy. Matthews himself ended up becoming an employee of HUAC as research director, a post he held for six years.

In fall 1939, as the peace movement was facing a critical turning point, HUAC sent its agents into the Washington office of the League without a search warrant. It removed the organization's membership and mailing list containing the names of over 500 people and released it to the press in October 25, 1939. Since a large number of those on the list were government employees, the obvious intent was to embarrass the Roosevelt Administration and intimidate federal workers. The President denounced the action as "a rather sordid procedure," quoted by Representative Martin Dies in *The Trojan Horse in America* (Dodd, Mead & Company, 1940). Among those on the list were Assistant Secretary of Interior Oscar Chapman, Mordecai Ezekiel of the Farm Adjustment Administration, and Edwin S. Smith of the National Labor Relations Board.

Addressing a protest meeting called by the Washington branch after the names of League members were released, Representative John Coffee (D-Washington) charged that the real aim of the committee was "to destroy the New Deal." He encouraged the League's members "not to be intimidated or terrorized by this so-called Congressional Committee." In the same vein, Harry Lamberton, the local chapter's chairman, who was an assistant counsel to the Rural Electrification Administration, protested HUAC's illegal invasion of the League's office to President Roosevelt and Attorney-General Frank Murphy. Since the League had consistently supported the President's domestic and foreign policy, we believed that the real purpose of the HUAC's actions against the League was to imply by association that New Deal policies were un-American.

Although the League ceased to exist by the end of 1939, many who worked in the peace movement were harassed long afterward. In April 1943, the House of Representatives, groveling before HUAC, approved an appropriations bill containing a specific provision barring payment of federal salaries to three government officials: Dr. William E. Dodd, Jr., employed by the Federal Communications Commission; Goodwin Watson, former Columbia University professor who was wartime analyst for the Federal Communications Commission's Foreign Broadcast Service; and Robert Morss Lovett, secretary of the U.S. Virgin Islands. The *New York Times* referred to this provision as the "bill of attainder," a reference to punishment without trial. All three men were charged with having belonged to the American League Against War and Fascism.

Meanwhile, the United States and the Soviet Union were now allies in the war against fascism. Ironically, the Congressional action accused the three men of having promoted the very alliance that became American policy. The Supreme Court eventually overturned the dismissal of the three officials as unconstitutional.

PART THREE

Everything Under Electric Lights

CHAPTER THIRTEEN

I Join the Trade Union Movement

In fall 1939, after a decade of working full-time in organizations dedicated to world peace and jobs, I went back to work in private industry. The "Fur Floor Boys" local of the Fur Workers Union directed me to a job at auction houses that sold raw skins. When I arrived, I saw thousands of pelts separated by species and country of origin. They were dangling from nails stretched along vast aisles, waiting for prospective buyers. A lone wolf hung near a string of rabbits. Newspapers advertised the rabbits as "coney."

It was my job to carry batches of skins to tables near windows where they could be examined in good light in preparation for auctions. Prospective buyers brushed the hairs back and forth, blew into them, and wrote bids in notebooks. I had been forewarned by auction house veterans not to be surprised if domestic dogs began following me home after work. Fortunately, no dog mistook me for raw meat.

My co-workers were mostly like myself, veterans of temporary jobs. Among them, I happened to discover Charlie O'Brian, a participant in the Catholic Worker movement led by Dorothy Day and Peter Maurin. They preached resistance to all wars and ran a center where needy and homeless people went for help. To the discomfort of the city's Catholic hierarchy, the Catholic Worker organization promoted the concept of common property. I enjoyed sitting with Charlie at lunch as we reflected on the evils of capitalism.

My career as fur bearer ended one Sunday afternoon when an iron bar used for securing a window dropped on my head. After emergency treatment at nearby French Hospital, the employer sent me to a doctor who limited his practice to worker compensation cases. In his midtown Madison Avenue office there was no stethoscope or other physician's instruments in sight. He explained that if I cooperated with him, I could get a lucrative settlement. Injuries on the back or head, he advised me, could readily be used for building compensation cases. No examiner at the state compensation office could refute a claim of persistent head or back pain. All I had to do was visit his office regularly. It was obvious that as the number of visits rose, his share of the potential compensation award would increase.

It became clear that the doctor was clearly seeking my compliance with a scam. I would benefit as well, but considering my meager earnings, not nearly as much as he would. After a few visits to his office where he did nothing but engage in idle talk, I insisted on settling the case without further delay. Eventually I was awarded an amount that covered just the days lost from work.

After the accident, I inquired at a local union office about a factory job. There was an opening at a Long Island plastics shop, but the union's business agent warned me that it was a "slave shop." Desperate for work, I took the job. It paid the federal minimum wage of 30 cents an hour, equal to $12 a week. Seven years before, I made $20 a week at the tailor shop.

My new job consisted of picking inch-long pieces of black plastic out of a barrel and placing them on a motor-driven shaft. Despite this grim work, the first day was a happy one because Gertrude gave birth to our son. When I visited her in the hospital at the end of the day, I could report that I had found work. Unfortunately, my new employer recognized my lack of commitment and soon decided he could get along without me.

About the time I left the plastics job, I received a request to prepare material for an issue on youth in a new weekly magazine called *Friday.* A staff of writers, photographers, and artists produced material on major issues confronting the country. Its first issue came out on March 15, 1940, as war in Europe was rapidly spreading, and the effects of the Great Depression were still much in evidence. In its issue of July 4, 1940, the magazine reported that of 21,000,000 Americans between the ages of

16 and 24, 6,000,000 were unemployed. Of the employed, according to a national survey, 45 percent believed that they were stuck in dead-end jobs. It was apparent that eight years of the Roosevelt Administration had not resolved basic problems facing young people.[55]

I was now 29 years old and father of a baby, seven months old. I needed to decide what direction to take. My upbringing in a union family, my experiences as an organizer during the previous decade, and my awareness of the rapidly growing industrial labor movement impelled me to become part of it. As I already had extensive experience writing for the peace and youth movements, I believed that I could contribute to labor as a journalist.

In 1940, I applied to the United Electrical, Radio, and Machine Workers of America for a job with its weekly paper, the *UE News*. I went to the office of Tom Wright,[56] the paper's managing editor, located at the Trade Union Service on Fifth Avenue. Although the union determined the policies and contents of *UE News*, it contracted out the mechanics of publishing to the Trade Union Service. The Service also put out publications for several other national CIO affiliates, AFL local unions, and the National Association for the Advancement of Colored People (NAACP). Several days after I met with Tom Wright, I received a telegram asking me to come to his office. This was the beginning of 44 years working for an organization whose principles I could support with total conviction.

Seventeen local unions had established UE in March 1936, at a convention in Buffalo, New York. At that time, 50 delegates represented over 16,000 dues-paying members. These proponents of industrial unionism and a new kind of comprehensive labor movement found a ready audience. In the past, an electrical manufacturing plant would have separate unions for electricians, sheet metal workers, carpenters, plumbers, machinists, pipe fitters, maintenance men, and more. Each of these craft unions affiliated with a different national union. Instead of encouraging worker unity in a plant, such craft unions ended up negotiating exclusively for their own members and reaching their own agreements. They sometimes went out on strike while other parts of a plant remained on the job.

This fragmented situation grew out of the AFL's belief at that time that only skilled workers could be relied on to be good union members.

Most unions were also prejudiced against minorities, working women and political movements that challenged prevailing social ideas. As mass production industries grew, this traditional approach to organizing left most workers in large plants outside of unions.

When I joined the staff of *UE News*, tens of thousands of workers were pouring into our union. The very first issue of *UE News that* I worked on carried a story announcing "10,000 more Join UE in the First Three Months of 1940." In the succeeding weeks our headlines ran:

"20th General Electric Plant Organized"

"Allen-Bradley Forced to Recognize Union"

"UE Wins GM Frigidaire Plant in Dayton"

"UE Recognized for 1,600 at Phelps Dodge"

"Monroe Calculator, Foster-Wheeler Sign"

"End Open Shop at Colt Firearms after 100 Years"

The massive corporate wall against unions, which only five years before seemed impregnable, was now being swept aside by a wave of industrial unionism. Industrial giants were facing a new twentieth-century labor movement. UE organizers were besieged with demands for assistance from workers far removed from the electrical industry. This led to our union's motto "We organize anything under electric lights."

When UE was asked to assist a group of workers outside the UE's jurisdiction, it was common practice for UE to help organize the group and find a suitable union with which it could affiliate. By February 1941, James J. Matles, director of organization, reported that UE had brought under a contract about two-thirds of the entire electrical manufacturing industry in the United States.

A set of principles virtually unprecedented in the labor movement supported the union's rapid growth. At the time, black workers were still specifically barred from membership in unions representing metal and electrical workers. Members of the International Association of Machinists actually took an oath to exclude them. The International Brotherhood of Electrical Workers and the Plumbers and Steamfitters were among the unions that barred them by tacit consent. In stark contrast, UE committed itself to organizing every worker in the industry regardless of "craft, age, sex, nationality, race, creed, or political belief."

Another major difference from most other unions was the principle that UE officer and staff salaries would not exceed the highest wages of workers in the industry. This principle was further refined by having annual union conventions approve increases for union officers in accord with salaries negotiated for workers at the General Electric (GE) and Westinghouse companies, where the largest number of union members were employed. When some other large unions were paying their officers from $50,000 to over $100,000 a year, corresponding UE salaries might be in the range of $20,000.

UE's organizational successes were being duplicated by other affiliates of the new CIO. Within months, more than three million workers joined the new unions. This phenomenal growth greatly added to labor's political influence and many unions, including UE, vigorously promoted political action. The Farmer-Labor Party in Minnesota elected governors, congressmen, and senators. In New York State, the American Labor Party ran its own candidates and supported the reelection of President Roosevelt in 1936. The Labor Party also helped elect congressional candidates friendly to labor. I was elected to the Labor Party's New York state committee several times and once ran unsuccessfully for state legislature.

Soon after I started working for *UE News*, I finally received compensation for days lost after being hit on the head by an iron bar at the fur auction house. I used the money to buy a used Zeiss Super Ikonta B with a Tessar lens, one of the best cameras made at the time. I began to study photography so I could illustrate my writing about the union. I had the good fortune to have as friends two skilled photographers. One of them, George Heyer, was later represented in the Museum of Modern Art collection "The Family of Man," and the other, Phil Stern, became a photographer in the movie industry. They let me hang around their dark room so I could observe how they developed their film. I then began processing film at home. I waited until the sun set and then hung black shades over the kitchen window.

I subsequently met a fellow member of the Newspaper Guild who worked at a Hearst newspaper. He earned extra money retouching photos for union newspapers at his employer's lab. He would stop by my home at midnight after his shift to pick up drying photos and have them processed the next day. I must admit, it gave me pleasure that the facilities of the notorious antilabor publisher were being put to good use by a moonlighting trade unionist.

My camera turned out to be invaluable to my reporting. Photographs and stories gathered in a union member's home added much greater depth to what I was able to report from picket lines. And because I came from the union, I was taken into the confidences of many people and could take photographs while they sat around a kitchen table or conversed with me on a living room couch. It was some time later that it became common for other labor press reporters to use cameras on their reporting assignments.

Sometimes employers would permit me to take pictures of workers at their jobs. However, I was turned down more often than not by employers who didn't want to have a union camera in the plant. A company that denied me the chance to use my camera would sometimes assign its own photographer to accompany me through the plant. The photographer would take the pictures I wanted and then send me the prints approved by the plant manager.

The burgeoning U.S. labor movement was acutely aware of the looming war in Europe and how it was affecting working people here and abroad. One month after I joined the staff of *UE News*, I wrote a series of three articles entitled "Why France Fell." These articles concerned one of the most shattering events of the time, the occupation of France by Hitler's army in the summer of 1940. The articles were a response to an attempt by American industry to use the press and huge billboards to blame the French defeat by the Germans on concessions made to French workers. American industrialists claimed that the 40-hour week in France, established two years before, caused a shortage of military equipment that enabled Hitler to overrun the country.

In the United States, the 1938 *Fair Labor Standards Act* (also known as the *Wage and Hour Law)* that established 40 hours as the normal work week in the United States was scheduled to go into effect on October 23, 1940. American industry, which had relentlessly fought against the eight-hour-day for more than half a century, was not yet reconciled to the law. They failed to stop its advance by every means they could devise, including the killing of workers by police during historic demonstrations in Chicago during the first week of May, 1886. Industry leaders now attempted to appeal to a misplaced patriotism to rekindle opposition. For example, the Merchants and Manufacturers Association of Los Angeles mounted almost 70 billboards using the French defeat by Hitler as a means to defeat the 40 hour work week. By this time, French employers had succeeded in replacing the 40 hour week with 60 hours and more.

Policymakers in Washington D.C. sat by while Italy conquered Ethiopia, while Japan overran China and fascists destroyed the Spanish Republic. *UE News* reported that in October 1940, according to the U.S. Department of Commerce, U.S. shipments to imperial Japan rose about one-third over the previous month, primarily in such essential war materials as gasoline, scrap metal and machinery. Our union paper vehemently protested this assistance, and an editorial denounced the demand by American arms manufacturers for a ten percent profit guarantee. The union claimed that a demand for such high guaranteed profits constituted blackmail. This was becoming very evident in light of military conscription in the U.S. and the military's urgent need for supplies.

Five years after those few dozen working people formed the union in 1936, *UE News* announced in May 1941, that the first national contract had been signed with Westinghouse on behalf of 50 thousand workers. The contract gave an unprecedented guarantee of seven to eight paid holidays annually. It further guaranteed paid vacations starting with one week after one year and going up to two weeks after five years. Having added 116,000 new members within a year, the union was in position to become a major factor in national affairs. At its national convention it made the commitment to support the evolving U.S. anti-fascist foreign policy. An editorial in the *New York Daily Mirror* (October 3, 1941) praised UE for negotiating difficult labor contracts without any major work stoppages involving military defense projects.

Our rapidly expanding union established its headquarters in a six-story stone building at 11 East 51st Street in New York, facing St. Patrick's Cathedral. The building once housed a branch of the Vanderbilt family. An unusual iron-grill door opened into a large foyer with Italian marble walls. A handsome curving marble stairway was once used as a backdrop by fashion photographers. The basement contained a room lined with niches for storing hundreds of bottles of wine. Cherubs decorated a ceiling on the second floor. It was in this room that the union held its board meetings.

In 1936, at 26 years of age, James B. Carey was elected president of UE during it's first convention. He came to the convention as representative of a local union at the Philco radio plant in Philadelphia. I met Carey several years earlier when he was a member of the National Council of the American Youth Congress, of which I was a founding member in 1934. I also knew him through his support of the American League Against War and Fascism, where I had been national youth secretary between 1933 and 1938. Carey was a forceful wielder of the gavel and a skilled debater.

The delegates at the first UE convention also chose Julius Emspak as secretary-treasurer. He was 30 years old and represented the Schenectady, New York, plant of the General Electric Corporation. His father was a GE worker who died in an accident at the Schenectady plant. At 16 years old, Julius got into the GE apprentice program, through which he attended engineering classes at Union College in Schenectady. He graduated from Union College, was elected to Phi Beta Kappa, and went on to study for a doctoral degree at Brown University in Rhode Island.

Emspak left academic life to rejoin the industrial labor movement, and went to work at the Radio Corporation of American (RCA) factory in Camden, New Jersey. At that time, it was owned by GE and was in the process of developing technology for television. His knowledge of the factory, his skills and working class background, and his total commitment to the labor movement led him to become a profound analyst of the challenges facing working people in their efforts to organize.

I first met Emspak earlier in 1936 when I was organizing support in the United States for the World Youth Congress in Geneva. I had gone to visit the UE office to encourage the union to send a delegate. The UE was then only a few months old and was already engaged in a tough strike at Camden, New Jersey, against RCA. Little did I know then that Emspak would later become a top official at UE when it represented hundreds of thousands of members, or that I would work together with him at the union for decades to come.

The day I entered the UE national office for the first time after I was hired in 1940, I ran into both Carey and Emspak. I was not aware that a bitter factional fight was building in the union with Carey and Emspak on opposite sides. The union had made a strong commitment to organize every worker in the electric industry without regard to political or other affiliation and to assure every member equality in every sphere, including the right to run for union office. However, in a column under his byline, Carey began using *UE News* to promote his differences with other officers over this policy.

At the heart of the controversy was whether UE would continue to allow workers with Communist Party affiliations to continue as members of the Union. Regardless of what anyone thought of communists, including their commitment to replacing capitalist society with socialism, their contribution to building the industrial union movement was well established. John L. Lewis, who had at first opposed communist influence in the Mineworkers Union, later called on known communists to help build the CIO. This call for assistance from party members acknowledged their long advocacy for industrial unionism and their extensive organizing experience.

Opposition to Carey was already building in the union for various reasons, including accusations that he was neglecting his duties as a union officer in order to promote himself elsewhere in the labor movement and in political circles. Representatives of the union at local GE plants asked him to keep out of their negotiations with the company because he had embarrassed them by disruptive outbursts. His erratic and contradictory positions concerning the union's fundamental principles led to his defeat as union president at the 1941 convention.

Albert J. Fitzgerald, a 34-year-old worker at the large GE plant in Lynn, Massachusetts, was elected to replace Carey. Fitzgerald proved he had the ability to deal with difficult and contentious issues in terms readily understood by union members. His defense of UE against the unrelenting attacks it was about to face in the next decades was critical to its future survival.

In 1948, Fitzgerald became co-chair of the Progressive Party's campaign to elect Henry Wallace to the U.S. presidency. Wallace's positions and those of the Progressive Party coincided with many UE policies, including workers' rights, civil liberties, ending racial segregation, and international relations. When the Progressive Party was defeated in the presidential election and failed to develop into a viable third political party, the labor movement lost a crucial historic opportunity to become an independent political force in national politics. Fitzgerald continued to be reelected union president at annual UE conventions and led the union for over three decades until his retirement in 1978.

Another leader who came into the UE at its beginnings was James J. Matles. He arrived in the United States from Rumania at 19-years-of age and found employment in a New York City machine shop where he joined the union movement. He was an imaginative organizer, a shrewd bargainer, and an exciting speaker. Under his leadership, several locals he helped organize into the Metal Workers Industrial Union became affiliated with the International Association of Machinists.

In 1937, Matles appeared as representative of the machinists union before a Senate Committee on civil liberties headed by Wisconsin Senator Robert LaFollette. Matles exposed the existence of a vast anti-labor spy network among metal workers. He and other organizers uncovered almost 40 company spies who were undermining union organizing efforts. In 1937, just a year after the founding of UE, the local machinists unions that Matles had first brought into the International Association of Machinists came into UE.

At the September 1937 convention of UE delegates in Philadelphia, the union officially became the United Electrical, Radio, and Machine

Workers of America. Matles was elected the first director of organization. In 1962, following the death of Julius Emspak, Matles was elected secretary-treasurer. He continued to serve as the union's primary spokesperson for more than a decade. He published a book with James Higgins about the history of UE, *Them and Us: Struggles of a Rank and File Union* (*Prentice Hall, New Jersey*, 1974).

Matles announced his retirement at the national UE convention in San Francisco in 1975. He was 65 years old. Following the convention, he traveled to Southern California where he had agreed to address a meeting of unorganized workers. He had mentioned to me during the convention that he was not feeling well enough to make the extra trip, but he felt obligated to go ahead with the commitment. After the convention, I flew back to New York to start work on the next issue of UE News. During the early hours of the following day, I was awakened by a telephone call. I was informed that Matles had died of a heart attack in his motel room in Santa Barbara. For three decades, Matles had stood out as one of the most forceful figures in shaping U.S. labor policy.

CHAPTER FOURTEEN

UE News

At home, my family was expanding. In March 1943, in the middle of world war, our second child, Betty, was born. Our son Richard had turned three years old. Starting a family during global conflict made Gertrude and I apprehensive over what the future would hold for our children.

Between 1941 and 1945, *UE News* vigorously promoted the union's commitment to the defeat of fascism. Our union members, employed as they were in a strategic industry, were experts in spotting weaknesses in the country's war production. They didn't trust corporate representatives or government agencies to put the country ahead of profit. A *UE News* headline announced that the union was offering the National War Board its plans for converting domestic refrigerator and radio production to war production. Whether there was a connection or not, the War Board soon thereafter ordered a halt to civilian products in the refrigerator industry.

Union representatives for 100,000 workers in 27 General Electric plants approved a proposal that union members give up all overtime pay for Saturdays, Sundays, and holidays during the war if the company would agree to turn the money over to the U.S. Treasury for the war effort. Although the company did not accept the offer, the union placed a full-page advertisement in *The Washington Post* explaining its proposals. The union's readiness to put patriotism before personal gain was widely recognized in the press and in Congress.

Based on its extensive knowledge of the machine tool industry, the union concluded at the beginning of the war that employers were utilizing only 65 percent of industry capacity. *UE News* described the union program for converting the machine tool industry to war production.

The union claimed there was an intentional corporate slowdown in such conversions in order to create shortages. The corporations thereby anticipated increased profits when the government would later require more war production.

UE News named specific factories that were not responding to the nation's defense needs. I myself investigated war production at the New Haven, Connecticut, Winchester arms plant. It employed 12,500 men and women in May 1943. The still unorganized workers charged that sloppy corporate production practices had caused the army to reject 10,000 carbines because of faulty parts. They told me of machines standing idle and of a large turnover of workers because of low wages in comparison to other similar plants. They described fatal explosions in the plants. This kind of information led a group of civic leaders in New Haven to set up a citizens committee to monitor the Winchester plant.

By 1943 more than 17,000,000 women, one third of the country's total production force, were drawn into industrial work. This was a jump of six million women in three years. Coupled with demands for equal pay for equal work, *UE News* stressed the urgency of programs to help women find time for household needs and child care. Later that year, a UE study showed that while the basic wage rates of industrial workers had been frozen at 15 percent above what they were two years earlier, the cost of living had increased by 35 percent. The study pressed for wage adjustments, a halt to price increases, extension of rationing, and better control over the quality of goods.

Since large numbers of the union's members were serving in the armed forces, the union initiated a campaign through *UE News* to encourage them to participate in the 1944 presidential and state elections by absentee ballot. The labor movement's efforts to persuade Congress to approve legislation for a simple federal servicemen's ballot had gotten nowhere. The union paper printed instructions on how people in the services could vote and informed them about which states offered absentee voting. From Italy, we received a letter in January, 1944, signed by 43 U.S. soldiers, thanking the union for helping make it possible for the armed forces stationed overseas to vote.

In April 1945, *UE News* marked the death of President Roosevelt with a detailed review of important legislation adopted during his leadership. The legislation included social security, unemployment insurance, the eight-hour day, 40-hour week, insurance of bank deposits, low-cost home mortgages, programs to rescue farmers from bankruptcy, rural electrification, and job creation programs.

The *Wagner Act* of 1935 protected the right of workers to organize and bargain collectively with employers. Following this historic legislation, the labor movement had grown to 12,000,000 members. Not only was the war coming to an end, but this was also an era in which, as never before in American history, a growing recognition of working people's needs was emerging. Summarizing the union's role in the war, *UE News* reported (August 8, 1945) that its members produced more than $17 billion worth of war material, equal to one-fifth of total United States war output.

The death of President Roosevelt presented the country and the labor movement with a vastly changed set of domestic and foreign policies. The president's Cost of Living Committee found that the cost of living had risen by over 43 percent from January 1941 to January 1944 and was still rising. This created a gap of more than 28 percent between the rise in living costs and wage adjustments. Unions were gearing up to overcome these losses, but it became clear that employers were determined to hold on to their huge wartime profits. The U.S. Department of Commerce estimated that corporate profits in 1946, after taxes, would reach $12 billion, compared to an average of four billion dollars annually between 1936 and 1939.

Betty Friedan

When I went to work for *UE News* in 1940, Katherine Beecher, a Vassar graduate, was also on the UE staff. She and editor Tom Wright met when she began working at the paper and later got married. Katherine was named for her great aunt, the sister of Harriet Beecher Stowe, author of *Uncle Tom's Cabin*. Beecher (as she preferred to be called) extended her work on the paper to bring more attention to women. She helped the wives of union members build an organization of their own, known at that time as the UE Ladies Auxiliary. This type of worker support organization was common in the labor movement and provided invaluable assistance to workers, both men and women, especially during strike activities when wages stopped coming in and workers were away from home for extended periods on picket lines. The women often helped set up and run strike kitchens, joined in the union's political action efforts and picket lines and took classes to understand union history and policies.

Another memorable associate I worked alongside in my early years with *UE News* was Betty Goldstein, later well-known as Betty Friedan, author of *The Feminine Mystique*, published in 1963. At the height of the union's growth during the war, *UE News* was putting out a 12-page weekly tabloid with a circulation of about half a million copies. In 1942, Goldstein, a Smith College graduate who had previously worked at Federated Press, a national labor press service, joined *UE News* as a reporter.

For many years, once a week, first Beecher and later Goldstein, would join me at a Greenwich Village printshop in early evening to wait for our managing editor, Tom Wright, to deliver a last-minute story or editorial. It was often long past midnight before we completed the paper's makeup and read the page proofs. After taking maternity leave in 1949 to give birth to her first child, Goldstein returned to *UE News* for another three years.

Goldstein and I frequently covered stories of broad national interest to union members, including equal rights for women in the workforce. She wrote a number of important articles on women's wages, among them several pieces on wage discrimination against women in the electrical industry.[57]

In 1952, a large decline in union membership took place at UE in the aftermath of the witch hunts of the McCarthy period. Both Betty Goldstein and Katherine Beecher were laid off during staff reductions. Professor Daniel Horowitz of Smith College noted in his book, *Betty Friedan and the Making of The Feminine Mystique* (University of Massachusetts, 1988, p. 141), that "Friedan later claimed that she lost her lost her job at UE when she was pregnant with Jonathan, her second child, because the union failed to honor its commitment to maternity leaves." Beecher, the other mother on staff with small children, had already used the union's pregnancy policy twice when she gave birth to her two children, as did Betty with her first child. Whatever Friedan's own memory was of her lay-off at the paper, my experience at the time was that all lay-offs were directly related to the drastic decline in the union's membership.

Sometime after Friedan left the employ of *UE News*, she came to its office in New York City and asked that her address be taken off the UE mailing list. She made it clear that she did not want to continue to be identified with UE during the McCarthy period by receiving mail from the union.

When Friedan later published her feminist writings beginning in the 1960s, she failed to credit her research and writing on women in the labor movement as a precursor to her books on feminism. She did not acknowledge that the struggle for women's rights in the labor movement and her own documentation of that struggle as a labor journalist at UE were important precedents to the American feminist movement in the twentieth century. Friedan's failure to credit the labor movement for its historic steps in securing women's rights later became the subject of renewed controversy and analysis. In the *American Quarterly of the American Studies Association* dated March 19, 1996, Daniel Horowitz discussed the controversy in an article entitled "Rethinking Betty Friedan and the Feminist Movement: Labor Union Radicalism and Feminism in Cold War America."

For myself and colleagues at UE who worked so closely with Betty on union and women's labor issues for many years, it was a loss to American history that a remarkable journalist and feminist leader failed to bring forward the seminal contributions that labor ideals and struggles had made to feminism in the twentieth century.

CHAPTER FIFTEEN

Cartoonists and Columnists

In 1949, a man appeared at the *UE News* office, introduced himself as Ed Hughes, and asked whether we could use a sports column. Everybody in the office recognized his name. He was a nationally syndicated sports writer who illustrated his columns with unique line drawings. He was also known as a "good union man" and was a founding member of the American Newspaper Guild when he was at the *Brooklyn Eagle.*

Hughes had served with General Douglas MacArthur's headquarters staff during the war as writer and illustrator. He was assigned to psychological warfare operations against the Japanese, including leaflets dropped from aircraft. After the war, he joined the organizing staff of the Oil Workers Union affiliated with the CIO. Ed brushed aside our concern that he might not want to work for our low UE salaries. He was committed to the principles UE stood for and that was enough for him. Besides, he was convinced that commercial publishers were blacklisting him for his union positions.

UE News proudly introduced Hughes to our readers. We reported that he covered every World Series from 1920 until he joined the army and had interviewed such great sports figures as Jack Dempsey, Joe Lewis, Red Grange, and Dizzy Deane. He had covered world chess tournaments and regaled us with tales that never saw the printed page. Not to be overlooked was the nickname he gave the Brooklyn Dodgers that afterwards clung to them, "the bums."

For 16 years, Hughes filled two columns of *UE News* with his finely-honed sentences. He was so precise that we never had to cut or add a word in order to fill the space allotted. He drew on his vast knowledge of the sports world to acquaint readers not only with the glory but also the corruption, commercialism and race discrimination in sports. At times, he would drop in at Jack Dempsey's restaurant a few blocks from the UE office and come back with choice morsels of sports lore from the former heavyweight champion.

The *New York Daily News*, the most widely circulated paper in the country at that time, offered Hughes a summer replacement job as editorial cartoonist. Ed turned it down because he felt his writing and drawing would have to conform to the paper's pro-business, anti-labor editorial policies. Instead, he stayed with the 35 dollar-per-column payment from *UE News* and took an extra job as a messenger on Wall Street.

The year that Hughes came to us, artist Fred Wright also enriched our *UE News* staff. He became widely known as a great labor cartoonist throughout the international labor movement. Like Ed Hughes, he had studied at the New York Art Students League. As a musician aboard cruise ships sailing out of New York, Fred had met seamen who were building the National Maritime Union in the early 1930s. His shipmates encouraged Fred to contribute cartoons to their union paper, *The Pilot*, and he later became its staff artist.

After Fred was drafted into the military in the Second World War, the army assigned him to draw for its publications. He returned to work for *The Pilot* after the war and gradually extended his field to other union publications, including *UE News*. His sharp wit enabled him to cut to the heart of complicated issues. When the cold war swept through the labor movement in 1949, Joe Curran, president of the Maritime Union, drove out most of the leaders who had built the union. Many ordinary seamen who refused to bow to McCarthyite restrictions were also forced out. Curran sought to persuade Wright to stay on with the maritime paper, assuring him that he would not be required to take sides in the split and would receive a generous salary. But when Curran directed Fred to draw a cartoon depicting the ousted leaders as rodents, the artist refused and was fired for insubordination.

Fred stayed with *UE News* until his death in 1984. It would not be an exaggeration to say that Wright drew tens of thousands of cartoons during that time. Many of them were picked up around the world in labor publications. At home, his work was used in publications of many unions and organizations that advocated for peace and civil liberties. Virgil Day, chief counsel for GE, was quoted as saying of Fred's work: "The cartoons are vile, insulting, outrageously offensive, but I have to admit they make me laugh." Fred and I collaborated on a cartoon-strip history of the struggle for the shorter work week. After the series ran its course in *UE News*, it was put into a pamphlet called *Telling It Like It Was* that was widely distributed.

Fred Wright cartoon from UE Calendar. (Courtesy of UE)

Another UE feature unusual in the labor press was a column written by Charles Kerns about radio and television programs. He came to the union after working in commercial broadcasting in Pittsburgh. He also put out general publicity for the union and worked with cartoonist Fred Wright preparing radio, television, and film scripts for local unions.

Above and beyond our ongoing reporting on union and international news, these original columns on sports and mass media, and Fred Wright's outpouring of cartoons, made *UE News* stand out among labor presses. As managing editor of *UE News* for 30 years, Tom Wright (no relation to cartoonist Fred Wright) would also often play a leading part in formulating written union positions based on policies adopted at annual conventions. Union president Fitzgerald would refer to him as our "fourth national officer."

Tom was an avid fisherman and hunter and took great pleasure talking about these subjects during his years with the paper. He was unhurried, both in his work and in his private life. When Tom decided to learn chess, he felt compelled to make his own chessboard out of fine woods, meticulously putting the pieces together. My brother Sol had installed a drill press and table saw in my Brooklyn attic. When I sought Tom's advice on making a dining table, he provided me with an unusual combination of gun stock finishing materials. It took endless hours of hand rubbing to work the wood down to the desired surface. Tom would generously participate in this operation during the stifling New York summer heat. When Tom Wright retired[58] I took on the post of managing editor of *UE News.*

CHAPTER SIXTEEN

I Cover the GE-Krupp Conspiracy Trial

A brief item in *UE News* of September 7, 1940, a few weeks after I joined the paper's staff, reported that two federal indictments were returned against the General Electric Corporation and the Krupp Armaments Works of Germany for conspiring to maintain a worldwide monopoly in production and sale of carboloy, a trade name for tungsten carbide. The government suspended its prosecution of the case at the outbreak of World War II. It was only seven years later at the war's end, that I began to understand the full significance of these indictments.

After the war in 1947, I spent months covering the trial of *U.S. v. General Electric Company, Fried, Krupp Aktiengesellschaft, E. T.* I heard both the testimony presented by the government and GE's defense arguments. The *Krupp Corporation*, whose offices were now temporarily under the control of the United States denazification authorities, was not called to testify. I told union members through a story in *UE News:*

> If you don't see anything about the GE-Krupp cartel trial in your local newspaper, don't be surprised. There's no one at most sessions of the trial to report it. One day there were two commercial newspapers and *UE News*; the next day, one commercial newspaper and *UE News*. Today only *UE News* was left.

I thereby sat there as the only reporter remaining to hear the full story of the partnership between GE and Krupp, its German partner. I could not help thinking what a field day the press would have had if union leaders were under criminal indictment instead of corporations.

After the opening days of the trial, I was also the only person in the courtroom who was not directly related in some way to the proceedings. I must have been conspicuous for my diligent presence, especially since I took extensive notes day after day. The defendants tended to ignore me even when I sat directly behind them to catch their comments. However, GE did not ignore what *UE News* would say about the case. Shortly before the trial was to begin, we ran a full-page story on the salient facts of the case based on the 160-page indictment. The company accused the union of printing "unproved charges of the indictments as facts" and of being antilabor because we were harming this great benefactor of the working man by printing such charges. This condemnation of *UE News* was distributed to all GE workers in the corporation's own newletter, *Work News* (February 7, 1947).

Far from innuendos, the facts that appeared in *UE News* came directly out of the hearings of the Senate Patents Committee held in April 1942 after the government obtained the indictments. At those hearings, GE was accused of being responsible for a "drastic shortage" of an essential material needed for manufacturing tools in the United States. This, the senators found, was in contrast with the situation in Germany, where the Nazis had an abundance of tungsten carbide. It was at these Senate committee hearings that one of the defendants, William G. Robbins, president of the Carboloy Company, a GE subsidiary, leaped to his feet and exclaimed, "I refuse to be called un-American or that our company is un-American."

One of the government witnesses at the trial explained how a tool edged with tungsten carbide could be used 1000 times before it had to be reground compared to only 100 operations using other tools. The indictment also cited tungsten carbide's superiority in parts for lathes, drills, saws, and other devices used in the production of military equipment and automobiles.

The U.S. government charged that in 1938 the American and German firms agreed to divide up the world market for carboloy. Before the agreement, the product sold for $48 a pound in the United States. After the agreement, GE set the price at $453 a pound or one dollar per gram. The prosecution showed that under the agreement, Krupp would control the sale of carboloy everywhere in the world except the United States and Canada, which were GE's turf. Government prosecutors refuted GE's claim that its expertise and patents were the sole reason this valuable material was available to American industry. The government brought to the witness stand a parade of businessmen who testified that they had been producing and selling tungsten carbide before the GE-German agreement went into effect.

Trial testimony showed that smaller competitors were either driven out of business or forced to go along with the price set by the monopoly. Methods used to accomplish this, according to witnesses, such as the president of the Union Wire Die Company, included forced buy-out of competitors. The head of American Cutting Alloys testified that he begged GE not to drive him out of business.

I was in the courtroom when a young man dressed in "army pinks" dragged in a heavy leather bag. For two days before being called to the witness stand, he guarded it carefully, even lugging it with him when he went to the men's room. The bag, it turned out, contained 13 folders from the secret files of the Krupp firm at Essen, Germany. Here was the actual record of the conspiracy dovetailing the documents the government found in GE's files. Company counsel had fought unsuccessfully to keep these records out of the trial. Charles H. Collison, chief of the metals section of the U.S. Office of Decartelization in Berlin, had previously informed the court that seven folders were missing. He told the court he believed these records were destroyed by the allied bombing of the Krupp Works.

General Electric defendants were visibly shaken when the witness opened the lock on his leather bag and began pulling out file folders. U.S. Attorney Malcolm A. Hoffman, who was in charge of the government's case, let me examine those documents in his office several floors above the courtroom. The memory of the war's horrors was still vivid in my mind as I read letter after letter from Krupp to GE officials ending with the phrase "Heil Hitler." I thought of concentration camp scenes that Allied armies had found in Germany, of the millions of people, including my own relatives, who disappeared forever into Hitler's death camps. By this time, the world knew that Krupp had run some of the camps where slave laborers produced goods for Nazi armies. In defense of its arrangements with Krupp, GE claimed that its tungsten carbide deal helped create jobs for American workers. Evidence showed, however, that the cartel arrangement actually resulted in job losses.

The government introduced the following documented message from Krupp to GE: "Understand that you are offering carboloy for export to Russia stop We point out you are prohibited from doing so. Krupp." When GE failed to satisfy its cartel partner, a harsher letter followed, concluding with an unspecified threat to GE (October 29, 1931). The threat had its desired effect, and in January, 1932, GE decided not to sell hard metal composition to The Amtorg Company, a Soviet purchasing agency. All this took place during the Great Depression when American workers were desperate for work. When Amtorg had advertised for 6,000 skilled American workers willing to take jobs in the Soviet Union, 100,000 people applied (*Business Week*, October 7, 1931).

Krupp was one of the German companies that notoriously financed Hitler's political career when he pledged to crush the labor movement before launching his drive across Europe. I was aware from trial evidence that even before Hitler came to power in 1933, Krupp had made its sympathies known with its "Heil Hitler" letters. Another letter from GE to a prospective customer, found in the files of both companies, dated April 18, 1940, read: "We are not permitted to sell tungsten carbide to China; you'll have to take your business to Germany." Rather than promoting employment as claimed at the trial, the cartel was in fact giving away American job opportunities to foreign workers.

GE's attempt to monopolize patent rights for tungsten carbide was undercut by a document found in its Schenectady files and presented as evidence. This consisted of a letter that was dropped into the company's suggestion box at its Schenectady, New York, plant by W. L. Merrill, an engineer in charge of the production of tungsten carbide. Merrill proposed that the material be sold for $50 a pound instead of the $453 set by the company. He wrote in the letter:

> ... a great deal of mystery has surrounded the production of this material since its inception. As a matter of fact, it is just about as complicated as making a good grade of concrete for a sidewalk. Grind up material, pass it through a mesh, put a certain percentage of binder with it, press it into a cake, and bake it.

Merrill went on to suggest that since the current actual cost of producing the product was $8 a pound it could be sold at his suggested price of $50 a pound, and still "give us approximately a 7 to 1 markup over manufacturing cost which should be a satisfactory profit." It started to become clear at the trial that while the company was boasting of its great patriotic service to the nation. it was charging an exorbitant markup for a strategic war material.

The evidence against GE became indisputable. As Judge Knox noted in his decision: "The defendants, by their counsel, have frankly admitted that they were monopolists and that they sought to prevent price competition." He found the company guilty as charged. He then practically apologized for making the verdict and sentence by stressing that since the offenses of which GE was guilty were eight or nine years old, he personally had "a very strong indisposition not to punish stale crimes too severely." The judge then turned down the government's request that the defendants be given a six-month prison sentence. Judge Knox imposed fines totaling $56,000 against the corporation and the individual defendants. He stated that a failure to impose any punishment at all "would be misinterpreted by many people." The government's attorney, at one point, stated that the business community regards fines in antitrust cases as "a license fee, which may be charged off as part of the cost of doing business."

In March, 1948, General Lucius Clay, United States military governor in Germany after the war, ordered a halt to the decartelizing of Germany's trusts. According to the *New York Times*, this had the effect of sparing "German industry any change in its corporate structure." (March 13, 1948). The following spring, Charles H. Collison, Deputy Chief of the U.S. decartelization branch in Germany, who provided the Krupp files to the carboloy trial in New York City, was fired. He claimed that he was being punished for giving an army investigating committee proof of the failure of American officials in Germany to carry out the antitrust programs that had been agreed upon by the United States, Great Britain, and the Soviet Union following the war.

Shortly before the tungsten carbide case had come to trial, the U.S. Atomic Energy Commission (AEC) began what it described as an investigation into the fitness of UE to represent GE employees at the corporation's Knolls Nuclear Energy Laboratory near Schenectady, New York. On the very week that Judge Knox was practically absolving the corporation of its conspiracy with the Nazi firm *Krupp*, the AEC directed GE to deny Knolls workers the right to be represented by UE. It claimed that the union presented a risk to the security of the United States. If this coincidence had been arranged in the corporation's public relations department to discredit the union, the timing could not have been more perfect. (*UE News*, October 11, 1948).

Having withheld the details of the GE-Krupp conspiracy throughout most of the trial, the *New York Times* carried on its front page a story about the AEC action against the union. The court verdict against GE, on the other hand, was reported on the entertainment page alongside advertisements. It was the height of irony that the very union that was praised by civilian and military leaders for its outstanding role in helping the United States and its allies defeat Nazism was now the enemy.

How did GE influence the press? One day at the carboloy trial, I saw defendant William G. Robbins reach into his pocket for his wallet and remove a clipping that he passed around to other defendants with obvious pleasure. Leaning forward, I could see that the clipping dealt with the indictment of Carl Marzani, who had made a film for UE called *Deadline for Action (1946).* The film offered an exposé of monopoly practices, including the tungsten carbide conspiracy. Marzani was tried and convicted on charges that he denied being a member of the Communist Party and had falsely signed a loyalty statement. He served 34 months in federal prison.

In the winter of 1957, I sat in for several days at another trial involving GE. This trial was in the same federal courthouse where I sat through the GE-Krupp case many years before. Now every seat was taken and all the trial details were extensively reported in the tabloids, with photographs and drawings. GE officials were accused of transporting prostitutes from New York City to Newark, New Jersey, to entertain prospective GE customers. At *UE News* we decided to ignore the story. The sordid activities of individual corporate executives seemed insignificant next to the great crimes of corporate monopolies during the war that were flagrantly ignored by the media and public leaders.

In 1961, GE and Westinghouse and some of their officials were found guilty of conspiring to rig bids on the sale of turbines. Following the verdict, attorney Malcolm A. Hoffman, who had handled the government's case in the tungsten carbide suit 11 years earlier and who had permitted me to examine the Krupp letters, wrote to the *New York Times. He* described how his request for jail sentences in the GE-Krupps tungsten carbide case had been rejected by Judge Knox. Hoffman noted that following that case, the United States subsequently brought 36 anti-trust suits against GE. In 1985, the corporation pleaded guilty to defrauding the government on missile-warhead contracts. This time, the court imposed a fine of $100,000 and $2 million in criminal and civil penalties.

CHAPTER SEVENTEEN

Historic Strikes

When World War II ended with the surrender of Japan the previous August, major unions agreed that it was time for working people to recover losses in earnings they had suffered because of severe wartime inflation. There had been almost a 50 percent rise in living costs since January 1, 1941. Now workers were no longer under a commitment to abstain from strikes.

I stood at the entrance to the big General Electric Company plant at Lynn, Massachusetts, on a fiercely cold day in January 1946, next to an energized line of people marching back and forth on the snowy pavement. I had arrived in this old industrial city north of Boston the day before to be on hand at dawn when the strike began. There had not been a strike of any kind at Lynn since 1918, when at the end of the First World War, a group of skilled workers struck after the company refused to raise wages.

Across the country, 200,000 workers in 78 factories of GE, Westinghouse and General Motors, in 16 states, were scheduled to strike that same morning. By more than an 80 percent majority, workers had voted to walk out, at a time called by UE, for a two dollar daily wage increase and paid holidays.

Within a few days of the UE strikes, almost all of the country's 800,000 steel workers were also on strike. A few weeks earlier, automobile workers went out on strike. Only a decade after their founding, these three unions within the CIO now constituted a powerful economic force. By the end of 1946, close to five million working people were out on strike.

The three major electrical manufacturing corporations rejected attempts to reach agreements with workers. Julius Emspak, the union's secretary treasurer, reported after meeting with GE president, Charles E. Wilson, that Wilson told him and two other UE officers present (President Albert J. Fitzgerald and Director of Organization James J. Matles): "The offer is ten percent or ten cents an hour. Take it or leave it." Emspak replied, "Mr. Wilson, in that case we'll just leave it." The same unacceptable proposal was put to the union by General Motors Corporation. The Westinghouse company did not even make the union an offer.

Ordinarily, night shift workers would have been streaming out of the Lynn plant at dawn. But that morning on the first strike day, there was no such exodus. Many third-shift workers did not go to work the night before in order not to violate the strike hour scheduled for five o'clock in the morning. Instead, they were out on the picket lines in the early morning.

As in most big strikes, the Lynn workers had to confront the problem of what to do about supervisory employees not covered by the union contract. Generally, strikers want to be assured that those not included in the collective bargaining unit will not do production work as scabs, thus weakening the strike's impact. At the same time, however, strikers had to consider whether denying the employer use of the supervisory staff would be used by the company as an excuse for seeking a court injunction. At their final pre-strike meeting, the members voted not to stop supervisors from entering the plant. However, they would not let them drive their cars in. Calls of "Let them walk," came from around the meeting. It was decided that supervisors would have to get walk-in passes from the union.

Now it was Monday morning and a man waving a letter from the company telling him to go back to work approached the picket captain. Pickets shouted, "Don't go in." As he turned and walked away, shouts of approval came from some of the pickets. On this day, the union and not the company held the power. So determined were the workers to show their commitment to the strike, they agreed not to go into the plant even to collect the last week's pay. Many women workers in their teens as well as older women who engaged in industrial work for the companies during the war walked the picket lines. They were fighting not only for the pay raise but also to support UE's position on equal pay for women. At the entrance to the union headquarters nearby, a young woman told me why she was on strike: "I don't even know what they're paying me. Every week it's something different. All I know is that I can't live on it."

Community support for the strike manifested itself in numerous ways. This caught the company by surprise, as we learned later from statements by its officials. A cobbler informed the union that he would resole the shoes of needy strikers and their families without charge. A pharmacist sent word that he wouldn't charge strikers for prescriptions brought to him. A group of local merchants sent a pledge of $10,000 for strike needs, thereby letting GE President Charlie Wilson know which side they were on. The union estimated that a pay increase of $2 a day would add at least $150,000 a week to the community's overall purchasing power. The local city council passed a resolution supporting the strike, and the mayor appeared at strike headquarters to show his support. Some local stores announced that they would not handle GE products for the duration of the strike and even took them off their shelves.

Meanwhile, among the more than 40,000 union members on strike in New England were several thousand Westinghouse workers in Springfield, Massachusetts. As I arrived there to gather news about the strike, local newspapers carried stories about women college students from Mt. Holyoke College who had walked the picket line the day before. We began to spread news about strike issues to the larger community and to thousands of college students in the area.

As news of the strike spread, people from other colleges began arriving at the picket lines. Among them were students from Smith College and the American International College. A decade earlier, I had toured New England colleges speaking about the war in Spain, and I was glad to see young people from these colleges now actively supporting the UE strike. They were getting a first-hand experience at labor struggles that no amount of classroom work could have provided them.

In Ohio, more than 37,000 workers at GE and Westinghouse struck, joined by workers employed at the electrical division plants of General Motors. It was at Lima, Ohio, that I had one of the most moving experiences of the strike. At union headquarters, Chet Schultz, a devoted union member at the Westinghouse plant suggested that I talk with Arthur Carroll, one of the strikers. Schultz felt that I could get a good idea of some of the conditions under which workers were living that impelled them to strike. We visited a couple and their two-year-old child living in a three-room shack that had no indoor toilet, no gas, and no drinkable water. As we entered this hovel I saw a batch of medical bills on the table. The father was a war veteran who had been wounded in the legs and was also afflicted with malaria. He spent extensive time in hospitals before returning to his job at Westinghouse. Now on strike, the family was without financial reserves to meet even daily expenses. Like other veterans of the war, they sought state aid. The welfare officer asked whether he was on strike and whether he belonged to the union. Incensed at the obvious attempt to subvert his support for the strike, Carroll refused to give them this information.

Other corporations under contract with UE where workers were on strike that year were such well-known corporate names as Pratt & Whitney in Connecticut, Anaconda in New York State and Allis Chalmers in Ohio, Pennsylvania, and Massachusetts. UE always considered calling workers out on strike as a last resort. When the wave of strikes swept through the electrical manufacturing industry and other basic industries, there were many employers, small and large, who decided to settle with their workers once the strength of the ongoing strikes became evident. The union was able to reach agreements without strikes at such companies as General Cable, RCA, Sylvania, Century Electric, Otis Elevator, Remington Rand, Philco, Stewart Warner, Columbia Records, and Allen-Bradley.

While most of the strikes did not produce violent confrontations between employer and workers, violent incidents occurred at the GE plant in Philadelphia and at Phelps Dodge in Elizabeth, New Jersey. Two weeks before the "big three" of the industry were struck by UE in January 1946, 2000 employees of Phelps Dodge Company at the New Jersey plant and several hundred more at a recently opened plant at Fort Wayne, Indiana, were already on strike. For two years, the union at the New Jersey plant had been trying in vain to get the company's president, Wylie Brown, to negotiate an agreement. Brown unilaterally nullified an existing labor agreement, refused to meet with the union, and rejected efforts of federal agencies to mediate the dispute.[59]

The Phelps Dodge plant was located on the waterfront and operated its own docks. Raw materials for the manufacture of cable arrived directly at the plant. These docks had been used early in the century for landing immigrants from eastern Europe who were seeking work. Among the men on the picket line on one of the days I arrived at the plant gate at Bayway, the city's waterfront, was a man who told me that he had worked at the plant for 37 years. His father worked there for 40 years before him. The Second World War and revolutions in eastern European countries had dried up that earlier source of labor. During the Second World War, black workers from the South began coming for the same reason as those who came earlier from Europe, to escape oppression and find work at better wages.

Despite previous gains workers had made at Phelps Dodge for a shorter work week, conditions at the plant lost little of their harshness and danger. Shortly before the strike began, a worker was crushed in a plant accident. On the picket line, I saw several men with picket signs held up by hands with missing fingers and other signs of industrial accidents. The plant was often referred to around town as "the slaughterhouse."

Unable to crush the strikers' spirit by refusing to negotiate with them, Phelps Dodge hired Anthony "tough Tony" Anastasia, president of a gangster-controlled local of the International Longshoremen's Association on the Brooklyn waterfront to find scabs to work at the plant. Anastasia was brother of the head of the notorious "Murder, Inc." Scabs moved across the bay from the Red Hook area of Brooklyn in two tugboats that landed at the docks fronting the plant. When union workers spotted them, they used two small crafts to go out and meet them and yelled for them to turn back. Nevertheless, many scabs managed to get into the plant from the water side. On land, meanwhile, pickets were prevented from approaching the plant by sturdy fences that had been previously erected for wartime security.

By July, the patience of strikers wore thin. Calling for reinforcements from other UE-organized plants in northern New Jersey, they carried out a plan to tear down the fences and get at the scabs who were using the waterfront landing as a sanctuary to come and go. As union workers reached the plant doors, they were met by a barrage of bullets. Phelps Dodge employee Bert Eckstein was wounded in the leg, and Mario Russo, a UE member from another plant, was shot in the neck.

As reports of the shooting spread through northern New Jersey, 10,000 workers stopped work for two hours in protest. Large numbers of workers came from other plants and shipyards to the Phelps Dodge plant in outrage. Within a few days, the company dismissed Anastasia and his scabs. They weren't around when the company called on the union to enter negotiations for a contract. Nine months after they walked out, the Phelps Dodge workers won the same 18.5 cent raise UE had already won months before at other major corporations. The company finally also agreed to establish a safety committee that would include union representatives.

As the strikers were voting to accept their contract, Mario Russo was undergoing a fourth operation at a Newark hospital. A delegation of Phelps Dodge workers visited him in the hospital to tell him they had won their demands. Mario later died, leaving a wife and four small children. He was twenty-seven years old. At his funeral on September 27, 1946, just 17 days after the strike ended, the Reverend Benedetto Pascale, pastor of the Baptist Church where Mario had worshipped, told the large crowd of mourners, "We are confused and bewildered when we think that this brother, Mario Russo, who volunteered his military service for our country and whose life was spared in war, should have returned home to be shot." Among the mourners that day were about 600 members of the union at Phelps Dodge who left work to attend the funeral. The company threatened to punish any workers absent from work to attend the services, and when the workers returned to their jobs, they were informed their paychecks would be docked.

After the strike settled, the state judicial system proceeded to put 16 workers on trial for having "incited to riot." They were out on bail as high as $5,000 each while Anastasia was freed on $2,500 bail for the fatal assault on the strikers. All union members were acquitted and so was Anastasia. Despite widespread appeals from the labor movement of New Jersey and many other sections of the population, Anastasia never suffered any consequences for the assault on the striking workers or for Russo's murder.

Union members walk off job to attend funeral of Mario Russo, killed during strike at Phelps Dodge plant in Bayway, New Jersey, September 1946.

Violence also broke out at a Westinghouse plant in Philadelphia. GE and Westinghouse sought, without success, to demoralize strikers at all their plants. The companies confronted striking union members with court injunctions and repressive police actions. An incident at Philadelphia brought national attention to these anti-union tactics. To protest a court injunction that severely limited the right to picket, strikers at the Philadelphia plant marched to City Hall to seek the mayor's support in getting the injunction withdrawn. They were joined by strikers at the South Philadelphia Westinghouse turbine plant. At the front of the line was a man named Dominick DiPerzio who carried an American flag.

Before organizing the march, union officers consulted with Police Captain Doyle, who assured them there was nothing in the injunction that denied them the right to march. This meant nothing to the police who were directed to stop the strikers from getting to City Hall. The following day, the nation's press carried a photograph showing a man lying on the sidewalk in front of a modest single-family home. Surrounding him were seven policemen on foot and one on horseback. The photographer caught one of the policemen in the act of swinging his club at the prostrate man, subsequently identified as Herb Lewin, a Westinghouse worker and UE member.

The photographer earned a prize for the picture of Lewin's beating after it was featured in *Life Magazine*. Another widely used photo showed police trying to wrest the American flag from DiPerzio. Eventually, many of the strikers made it to City Hall to plead for the right to engage in peaceful picketing, but the mayor ignored the appeal. GE strikers urged company president, Charles Wilson, to dissociate the company from this violence. Instead, Wilson issued a statement that Philadelphia police used force against the strikers only in self-protection. It was an obvious falsification of what had happened, as demonstrated by the testimony of witnesses and the many photographs showing police using unnecessary force.

Police arrested 16 marchers and charged them with rioting. After the strike was settled, workers appealed to the company to use its influence to get charges dropped. Instead, GE sent a letter to every employee at the Philadelphia plant proclaiming that "the issues are whether or not force and violence and anarchy are to predominant over the laws." It was highly ironic for a corporation whose files included an extensive list of antitrust violations, convictions, and pleas of "no contest" to put on the guise of upholders of the law.

At the trial of the arrested union members I listened while about 50 policemen and detectives spun tales about what happened during the strike the previous February. Despite viewing photographs of unarmed workers being beaten, the police insisted that nobody was beaten that day. Under cross-examination by a union attorney, one officer admitted that he had "picked up at random three or four people" and arrested them. The cynicism of the state's witnesses was exemplified by a policeman who swore that the worker who had struggled to hold on to the American flag was beaten up by one of the union leaders. At this, I saw several of the policemen at the trial laugh out loud.

Many witnesses appeared on behalf of the workers, including an American Legion commander, a court officer, businessmen, and schoolteachers who knew the defendants. The most effective witnesses were several working women who lived near the GE plant where the marchers were assaulted by police. One courageously agreed to testify on behalf of the union. Police chased strikers onto her porch and it was on the sidewalk in front of her house that the prize-winning photograph was taken of policemen beating the prostrate union man.

All the union members were found not guilty even though, during the jury selection process, the district attorney ensured that no juror belonged to a union. It took the jurors only an hour and a half to reach its acquittal verdict. While I read extensively over the years about court cases against labor that were constructed on perjured testimony, and I was present at many of those trials, this was the first time I had witnessed a blatant frame-up. Fortunately, the atmosphere in the country at that time made it possible that a powerful corporation could no longer totally dominate the courts.

CHAPTER EIGHTEEN

The Enemy

The era of the 1940s and 1950s can be summed up all too well in the phrase spoken by GE president, Charles E. Wilson, to U.S. President Harry S. Truman in 1946, concerning the main targets of corporate attention: "Russia abroad and labor at home." This pronouncement foretold the direction the country would be taking for decades to come as large corporations promoted the cold war and the nuclear arms race and at the same time attempted to weaken the growing U.S. labor movement. Successful efforts were made to fragment the union movement and pass legislation that would drastically reduce workers' rights to organize.

The corporate battle against labor was often fought in the name of stopping communism. The National Association of Manufacturers leapt into the crusade with a widely circulated pamphlet entitled "Join the CIO and Build a Soviet America." But there was a much bigger aim, which was to reverse labor's growing national influence that had begun in 1933 with the Roosevelt administration. Again, it was an official of GE who made this clear. Soon after the 1946 strikes, Lemuel R. Boulware, corporate vice president for GE, stated:

> Communism and other forms of collectivism are pressing on all fronts towards the destruction of America and its economic system. They are hammering from without and boring from within toward the substitution of a form of big government and little people for our traditional minimum of government and maximum of free individuality. (*Editor and Publisher*, the trade publication of the newspaper industry, November 6, 1948).

Boulware complained that because of the "collectivists," employees became dissatisfied with their jobs and felt "distrust and dislike for employers and for the economic system itself." He reported that a GE company official was helping the Lions Club in Schenectady, New York, run a course for more than 400 businessmen on how to spread the anti-communist message. He called on the advertising industry and corporations to spread this message to the entire country. This heavy-handed approach became widely known as "Boulwarism."

In 1947, the National Association of Manufacturers promoted the addition of a provision to a bill in Congress to amend the *National Labor Relations Act* of 1935. The purpose of the amendment, known as the *Taft-Hartley Act*, was to limit the right of labor to organize. Senator Robert A. Taft, Republican from Ohio, claimed that the amendment satisfied "about three-quarters of the matters pressed upon us very strenuously by employers." It had the effect of encouraging employers to seek court injunctions against unions, sue unions for alleged damages, and intimidate workers in plants where union organizing efforts were taking place.

A provision of the *Taft-Hartley Act*, which Congress passed over the vehement objections of the labor movement, gave the National Labor Relations Board (NLRB) authority to deny workers the right to freely choose their own union officers. It required candidates for union offices to sign affidavits swearing that they were not communists. Refusal of candidates to sign such an affidavit became grounds for denying a union the right to participate in elections to choose collective bargaining representation. As a result, union members holding office or desiring to seek office had to think about the consequences of having someone charge them with perjury if they refused to sign the affidavit.

Initially, there was strong support in the labor movement for nullifying the *National Labor Relations Act* simply by boycotting it. A convention of the United Steelworkers Union declared, for example, that the union would "resolve all issues between our union and the employers through bona fide collective bargaining and other peaceful means wherever possible, instead of seeking the intervention of the Labor Board." United Mine Workers President John L. Lewis, who played an important role in establishing the CIO, refused to bow to the affidavit. While Lewis fought communist influence in the mine union for years when he helped form the CIO, he refused to accept a government decree that would limit workers' choice of who could represent them.

James J. Matles, UE secretary-treasurer, warned delegates at the 1947 CIO convention that they could not simultaneously keep denouncing the *Taft-Hartley Act's* anti-communist affidavit while lining up to accept it. He pointed out that the injection of the spurious issue of communism into the *Labor Relations Act* had created a weapon by which employers could finally set about destroying effective unionism. Eventually the U.S. Supreme Court ruled in 1965 that the anticommunist affidavit provision of the Taft-Hartley Act was an illegal bill of attainder and therefore unconstitutional. However, the decision came far too late to prevent the irreparable damage that had already been wrought upon the union movement.

As European governments lined up to support the cold war, it became increasingly profitable for American corporations to move operations abroad. The North American Philips Corporation announced in 1948 that it was moving its Dobbs Ferry operations to Europe because devaluation of European currencies made it cheaper to produce TV sets and electric shavers in Europe. There was sad irony in this for the employees at the New York plant. Shortly before the plant closed, the AFL's machinists union had persuaded workers to change unions with the claim that UE was communist-dominated.

While UE continued for a long time to hold to its refusal to surrender to *Taft-Hartley*, other unions that had at first expressed opposition soon began to capitulate to it. Among the very first to do so was the United Automobile Workers (UAW) under the influence of Walter Reuther, who was engaged in a factional war to take over his union's leadership. He asserted that his opponents, including many of the union's founders, were under the sway of communism. He also led a drive to break off groups of workers organized by UE in order to bring these workers into UAW. In 1948, workers at the Royal Typewriter plant in Hartford, Connecticut, and the Mergenthaler Linotype Company in New York City, were persuaded to leave UE as part of the anticommunist crusade. Ironically, before becoming director of this crusade, Reuther had once advised union members that when bosses who "peddle the red scare" call a union leader a "red, they mean ... he is a loyal, dependable union man...." (William Kampelman, *Communist Party vs CIO: A Study in Power Politics, Frederick A. Praeger, 1957.*)

At a luncheon meeting in February, 1949. of the National Industrial Conference Board at the Waldorf Astoria Hotel in New York, I heard GE officer Boulware tell several hundred representatives of industry that the "greatest peril" facing employers was the fact that unions were winning wage increases from small companies. He warned that this was setting a pattern the bigger employers could not withstand for long. I could not help thinking to myself how this was the very strategy that UE had used for years to bargain for higher wages. Even more significant to me were Boulware's remarks that GE regarded the implementation of the *Taft-Hartley Act* as the highest priority for industrial employers. He called for corporations to pressure Congress to retain the non-communist affidavits.

Between the passage of the Taft-Hartley Act in 1947 and September 1949, UE was subjected to more than 450 attacks by other unions seeking to appropriate sections of UE into their organizations. UE's financial and organizational resources were largely diverted from its primary task of organizing and protecting workers, to that of defending itself from destruction. In this unprincipled and unprecedented cannibalism, employers had the support of the media, local, state and federal officeholders, and courts and government agencies. It was a tribute to UE's achievements that in little over a decade since its birth anything remained of it at all.

UE refused to attend the 1949 CIO convention after withholding dues to that body as a protest against CIO efforts to break up existing unions and its support of the *Taft-Hartley Act.* The convention went on to oust 11 unions from the CIO, including UE. These unions represented 20 percent of the affiliated membership of the CIO. All had refused to accept the *Taft-Hartley Ac*t and were critical of the government's cold war politics. Completing this act of self-destruction, the CIO convention voted to authorize and finance the establishment of a rival electrical workers' union to displace UE.

The officers of the CIO chose James B. Carey, defeated for reelection as UE president in 1941, as president of the newly created electrical workers' union. This union took the name International Union of Electrical, Radio and Machine Workers (IUE). Carey's CIO sponsors provided him with funds to destroy UE. This was the first time in American labor history that a union was set up for the express purpose of destroying a functioning, highly successful existing union.

The chartering of a new union by the CIO was the result of the failure of Carey's supporters to regain control of UE at its 1949 convention. At that emotion-charged gathering, Secretary-Treasurer Julius Emspak accused the Carey group of trying to turn the union into an organization devoid of militant labor organizing. He strongly condemned corporate Cold War policies. Unlike his fellow officer, Director of Organization James J. Matles, whose oratory could transfix audiences, Emspak was not given to oratorical flourishes. Yet after he spoke these words everyone there realized they were witnessing a historic turning point, not only in the life of UE but also, given UE's size and influence, in the entire labor movement.

If proof of Emspak's evaluation of Carey's motivations were needed, it came inadvertently from a GE official, W. V. Merrihue, who revealed shortly afterward that "Jim Carey ... came to us before the last convention [of the UE]. He apparently wanted to get our help in breaking the commie hold on the union." UE also learned that Merrihue told a group of company officials that the endeavor "to get out from under the domination of the left-wing UE" would be consummated that year. This was 1949, the same year that the CIO had expelled the 11 unions, including UE, thereby launching a debilitating internal struggle within the labor movement.

Under the *Taft-Hartley Act*, as under the *Wagner Act*, a contract between a union and an employer assured that the union's certification as collective bargaining agent remained in effect until the contract expired. This left the Carey group with much publicity and no members, because UE had already negotiated two-year contracts that were still in effect. Rushing to the rescue, GE, Westinghouse, and scores of other corporations professed to have no knowledge of which workers UE represented in their plants. They urged the NLRB to help them out. The Board obliged by decreeing that if there is a "schism" among a plant's employees, a contract would no longer be a barrier to holding an election to determine which union should be recognized.

Two years later, the same GE official, W. V. Merrihue, stated: "We took Mr. Carey off the hook by filing our own petitions for an NLRB election. This under NLRB rules made it unnecessary for the IUE-CIO to show any membership at all. The president of Westinghouse also claimed credit for being one of the first companies to support IUE and file petitions with the NLRB calling for new union elections. It became clear that the "schism" ruling of the NLRB was invented to dismember UE and the ruling was in fact never used again. Meanwhile, it became impossible for UE to defend itself against competing unions that had capitulated to the *Taft-Hartley Act.* UE was finally compelled into accepting the signing of anticommunist affidavits in order to even participate in union elections. UE thus became the last CIO union forced to accept *Taft-Hartley.*

The mere filing of petitions for a NLRB election to determine whether union members wanted to continue to be represented by UE would not have attracted much attention. However, the filing actions were accompanied by a barrage of anticommunist propaganda and firings of workers who supported the union. Washington politicians threatened to deprive companies of contracts if UE continued to represent workers.

General Electric and Westinghouse in fact had good reason for wanting to get out of its contracts with UE. Between 1936 and 1959, the union negotiated significant wage increases at those corporations, established the first paid holidays and paid vacations for production workers in major industries, and established time and a half payment for Saturday work and double time for Sundays. UE initiated major efforts to eliminate discrimination against women and black workers that was up to that time a routine practice in large electric corporations. In the cold war atmosphere that prevailed in the country, it was much easier for corporations to vaunt their virtues as opponents of the left wing than to continue to negotiate with a union that had been successful in winning wage gains and benefits.

While corporations were assisting the still memberless new Carey union by requesting union elections, leading politicians, including President Harry S. Truman, were also urging workers to reject UE. By the time the first round of elections was completed, UE was severely weakened. As a result, the ability of workers in the electrical manufacturing industry to defend themselves from employer policies, regardless of which union they were in, was sharply curtailed. UE, which had reached a membership of nearly half a million during the war, was now reduced to about ninety thousand. Sharp cutbacks in the electric industry following the end of the war accounted for much of this decline, and strong union efforts were needed to protect workers' gains. The IUE, the union that was set up to replace UE, had little reason to organize the unorganized because it was fulfilling its mission of breaking apart UE.

Despite attacks from all sides, UE remained a force in the industry. In 1953, UE petitioned the NLRB for an election at the Lynn, Massachusetts, GE plant to bring workers back into the union who had been split away three years earlier. Local newspapers announced the election:

> Coming almost simultaneously with the Washington decision [to hold the election] was an announcement in New York last night by Senator Joseph McCarthy (R-Wisc.) that he and his Senate Investigating Committee will hold a closed hearing in Boston tomorrow at 11 A. M. on security policies and alleged communist infiltration at GE's Lynn and Everett plants.

Two eight-column streamers ran across the top of one local newspaper: "NLRB Orders GE Union Poll," and under this, "McCarthy Due to Quiz Lynn Workers on Red Ties."

GE President Ralph Cordiner announced that the company would immediately suspend employees who refused to testify under oath. IUE denounced UE as "red-led," and Carey gave the Massachusetts press a list of 200 alleged communists in UE. He urged the NLRB to bar UE from participating in union certification elections. Carey knew of course that there was no legal basis for such action, but it was just one more way of getting headlines at a time when a UE victory was still possible. Meanwhile,

McCarthy was holding hearings to intimidate workers and the public. GE was set to fire anyone who refused to be a party to this outrageous assault on workers' rights.

James J. Matles, UE director of organization, boldly took the offensive against Senator McCarthy, whose wild charges against broad sections of government, labor, science, and education had been terrorizing the country. Matles demanded that the senator allow him to appear at the hearings to answer the attack on the union. He defended his own loyalty and the union's loyalty to democracy. The hearing at the federal courthouse in New York City came to an abrupt end when Matles denounced the senator for his anti-union tactics. McCarthy demanded that the government immediately begin deportation proceedings against Matles, who came to the United States from Europe as a teenager. Although the deportation process ultimately failed, it was used at the time as another insidious means to discredit the union.

The 1954 McCarthy hearings in Boston were widely reported in the press and spurred fear and suspicion in the community of workers at the Lynn GE plant. Immediately after the hearings, the company carried out its threats to fire workers with many years of service who had defied the McCarthy investigations. GE feared that if UE won, the company might be denied government contracts. On the eve of the scheduled election, Senators John F. Kennedy (D-Mass.) and Hubert Humphrey (D-Minn.) announced their endorsement of IUE, the opposing union. When the Lynn vote by union members for a collective bargaining unit finally took place, UE failed to win by only a couple of hundred votes out of a total of 13,000 votes. It was a tribute to the union's achievements that thousands of men and women still defied such an unprecedented affront to their democratic rights by continuing to vote for UE in such large numbers.

Another McCarthy committee meeting challenged the loyalty of UE's leaders at the Westinghouse Electric plant in East Pittsburgh, Pennsylvania. Seven of the local union's top leaders were fired after a McCarthy committee session. The application of the Cordiner "doctrine" of either surrendering-your-democratic rights or be fired was used by GE to rid itself of John Nelson, the able president of UE at the Erie, Pennsylvania plant. At a 1953 court hearing to contest the Nelson firing, the McCarthy committee did not deny that it had met with GE officials in the fall of 1953 and influenced the company to discharge any workers who failed to satisfy the committee's questions.

Among the other pressures UE members had to withstand was interference from an organization calling itself the Association of Catholic Trade Unionists, led by Father Charles O. Rice of Pittsburgh. He distributed a twelve-page manual detailing methods to be used in disrupting UE meetings as part of a plan to take control of the union. On the eve of the Labor Board election in Erie, where workers were to vote on whether to remain in UE or join IUE, a local clergyman publicly berated Catholics who supported UE, warning them that a vote for UE was "a vote against God." Never before had there been such an intensive effort to inject clerical influence into the American labor movement. Schools and classes led by Catholic clergymen were set up across the country to provide training on how to capture union offices based on issues tied to cold war politics.

Over a decade later in 1966, Rice recanted his campaign against UE during the fifties. In the *Pittsburgh Catholic*, he expressed regret at the role he played in anticommunist attacks on the union. It was a great irony that Rice came to this change of mind through his opposition to the Vietnam War, because opposition to the war was a position taken by UE from the beginning of the Vietnam conflict.

In an oral history project at Penn State University, Rice recognized that the destruction of UE was tragic for the labor movement. He admitted that the communist threat was "exaggerated out of all proportion," and referred to UE as one of the best American unions. (See *The Communists and the Communist Issue in the American Labor Movement 1920-1950*, unpublished Ph. D. dissertation by James R. Prickett). Rice's Catholic trade union organization disbanded not long after it played its historic part in splitting UE from the CIO. In 1973, I clearly saw Rice appear at the door to the UE convention hall in Pittsburgh and then approach President Fitzgerald. I watched as the two spoke briefly. It turned out that Rice had come to personally express regret for his part in the huge losses the union suffered during the McCarthy era.

During the 1950s, industrial employers who claimed that grievances and strikes had hurt company profits were supported in these claims by a major sector of the labor movement. These were the unions that equated militant unionism with the work of saboteurs and agents of Moscow. When U.S. intervention in the Korean War in 1950 stimulated a wave of inflation, the Truman Administration set up a Wage Stabilization Board on the theory that working people were causing inflation by buying too much. To control inflation, the Board set out to minimize the amount of money available for spending by imposing a wage freeze. In support of this policy the UAW committed auto workers to their first long-term five-year agreement with General Motors.

UE and other aggressive trade unions always held that such long-term agreements were in the employer's interest and were unfavorable to workers. *Business Week* noted that "GM has bought five years of comparative labor peace. Its workers, with nothing to fight over for the next half decade save minor grievances will almost forget they are union men." UE recognized that its members would be hurt by a government-induced wage freeze and that it would cause workers' share in profits to go into a steady decline. The union appealed unsuccessfully to CIO and AFL leaders to reconsider their endorsement of the freeze.

Secessions

Two major assaults on UE occurred between 1950 and 1956. The first was carried out in the name of fighting communism. The second came from the Communist Party itself, following the merger of the AFL and CIO in 1955. The Communist Party viewed the merger as an important opportunity for the rebirth of labor strength at a new national level that all unions including UE could support. However, UE opposed joining the AFL-CIO merger because our union was gaining more for its members through its own bargaining strength. It also wanted to maintain its much more democratic structure that included more participation by local union members. After failing to convince UE leaders to join AFL-CIO, the Communist Party turned to encouraging UE members to leave the union. Hardest hit by member loss to other unions were UE's organizations in New York, New Jersey, Ohio and Michigan.

The great redudtion in UE's membership, caused first by the McCarthy hearings and later by Communist Party efforts to break up the union in favor of the AFL-CIO merger, had devastating effects on the union's bargaining strength. The weakening of UE's force in the 1950s clearly showed in statistics. When a Washington lobbyist for GE addressed a meeting of the American Retail Federation in November 1960, he noted that in 1946 (the year of the historic strike against GE), almost all of GE's hourly workers were members of UE. In 1960, only 30 percent of the company's workers were organized into unions and GE was now dealing with over 90 different unions. After the calamitous dispersion of the union movement that resulted from the great schisms in the labor movement during the 1950s, labor agreements consisted primarily of corporations informing unions what it was willing to grant workers in the way of wages and benefits.

Secessions in the membership of UE were deeply felt by union officers and staff. Our union had gained widespread respect for overcoming antilabor tactics carried out by the country's most powerful corporations. Now this monument to labor idealism was being torn down in front of our eyes. We were simultaneously experiencing great personal losses. This was especially true in 1956. Many who stood up to the worst McCarthy era attacks on the union and withstood physical violence and prison were now persuaded, along with thousands of other UE members, to desert the union at the urging of the Communist Party. Close friendships were destroyed in the heat of conflicts that arose. Personal friends at GE and Westinghouse told me outright that if I came to speak to the union locals to object to their leaving UE they would throw me out. A UE organizer who went to a Westinghouse plant was threatened with physical violence by people who walked with him on many picket lines and defied years of anticommunist persecution together.

As a journalist for UE News, I attended IUE conventions with obvious trepidation. In IUE publications, distributed by the hundreds of thousands of copies at factory gates, UE was literally depicted as a nest of foreign agents. Even my participation in the prewar peace movement against Hitler became an example in this compendium of a suggested foreign influence in the UE. A leaflet distributed during the Korean War showed a photograph of UE President Fitzgerald alongside a field of crosses depicting the Korean War death toll of 140,000 American soldiers. Dripping pools of blood surrounded the crosses. And here I was, at their convention, a reporter for the union that was supposedly promoting all these despicable crimes against the United States.

At these IUE conventions, I ran into many men and women I had known for years at UE. They would greet me and often express regret at having been led out of the union. At the IUE convention in St. Louis in 1956, president James B. Carey, former president of UE, came down from the platform, approached the press table, and greeting me warmly, suggested that I "come over." By way of encouragement he mentioned by name several former local and district officers of UE who were influenced by the Communist Party's effort to dismantle UE and join the mainstream AFL-CIO merger in 1955. Carey had of course played the ignominious role of helping split apart the most effective union ever built in the electrical manufacturing industry, and of contributing to the general decline of the American trade union movement. I rejected Carey's invitation, not failing to mention the undemocratic practices of his organization.

In 1968, 13 years after UAW president Walter Reuther had played such a decisive part in consummating the merger of the AFL and CIO, he severed his union's relations with it. He charged it with failure to organize the unorganized; failure to develop a collective bargaining program to meet workers' needs; failure to fight for equal rights for all working people; and with failure to have a peace policy worthy of the labor movement because of the AFL-CIO support for the Vietnam War. Three years later Leonard Woodcock, who succeeded Reuther as president of the UAW following the latter's death in a plane accident, told a UE convention that "labor needs to pull together as we have never pulled together before." The labor movement, however, could not so easily be glued back together after years of unrelenting attacks and secessions.

By the late 1960s, economic pressures on the divided labor movement in the electrical industry and changes in leadership, made it possible for the unions to join forces again. UE and IUE finally began facing the corporations together, and joined in a common strike against GE in late 1969. The strike lasted 102 days and led to the first negotiated collective bargaining agreement for UE in 20 years.

CHAPTER NINETEEN

Silica Dust

Faces, arms and clothing covered with soot, groups of workers left the General Electric Company foundry at Elmira, New York on a warm June day in 1948. They crossed the street, entered and then left a large tent. This procession went on throughout the day until nearly 700 workers made the trip. Thus began an intensive union effort to save these workers from silicosis, the irreversible and deadly lung disease caused by long-term inhalation of silica dust. The condition is similar to "black lung" disease among coal miners and "brown lung" among textile workers.

UE holds medical testing for workers employed by a GE plant in Elmira, New York, in June 1948. Union negotiations subsequently achieve regular testing by GE for silicosis as part of the union contract.

Three months earlier, several of these afflicted workers came to the UE national headquarters in New York City to report that the New York State Workmen's Compensation Board had found that some of the foundry employees had become permanently disabled with silicosis. The source of the problem was the company's method of producing castings. Union pressure persuaded the company to make some improvements over the years but much more remained to be done. UE undertook to force the company to take necessary action by making silicosis a public issue and by engaging Dr. Saul Solomon, a New York City specialist in lung disease, to work with the union.

In preparation for a story on Elmira, I visited Dr. Solomon at his office. He detailed how silica dust irritates the lungs and then causes scar tissue to form over the abraded spots. This process results in frequent colds, influenza, and pneumonia. As breathing becomes more difficult, the heart gets overtaxed. The condition affects even ordinary activities, such as walking short distances. In extreme cases, the disease results in lung hemorrhages. Dr. Solomon said that silicosis could be mistakenly diagnosed as tuberculosis. However, tuberculosis was a disease for which workers could not receive employee compensation and a company could easily claim that tuberculosis had been contracted elsewhere.

The union's plan called for every foundry worker to be given a chest X-ray with a follow-up examination for those suspected of having silicosis. As they entered the huge tent, workers were registered by their local union officers, who recorded their employment history and other information needed by the physician. The workers often expressed gratitude for the chance to be examined by a doctor and technicians hired by the union. Many were convinced that doctors hired by the company were cooperating with the employer to downplay the health impacts of silica dust.

I saw what actual conditions these men worked under when I went to the foundry. In *UE News* the following week, I reported:

> A group of men stand around a machine. They are shaking out a casting elevated high above the floor. Suddenly they disappear in a cloud of black dust. Some of the dust falls to the floor, some obviously enters their lungs. Around the floor of the foundry, you kick up several inches of dust

> as you plod through the core-making and mold-making departments. These cores and molds are made out of raw sand, the stuff that contains silica that grinds men's lungs (June 1948).

According to a GE publication given to plant visitors, castings ranging from a fraction of a pound up to as much as two tons were turned out during foundry operations. To find out if there was a less hazardous way of doing this job, I consulted a company engineer who asked to remain anonymous. He told me that other companies had already done away with the conditions still being imposed on the Elmira workers. It soon became a union priority to compel the company to institute safer methods.

The first X-ray session in the tent showed that as many as 90 men out of 700 already had some scarring of the lungs. The union arranged for that group to undergo a second series of tests and receive individual physical examinations. Of the men who were found to have some scarring, the doctor judged that ten had severe cases and the others "moderate" or "mild" cases. Since silicosis is irreversible, even a mild case became a lifelong medical burden.

After company management dragged its feet on ending hazardous conditions leading to silicosis, the union put its case before the public. A union advertisement in the *Elmira Star-Gazette* (November 23, 1948) in the form of an open letter to the plant manager stated that so many months had passed since the union first took up the matter of silica dust with the company, that workers were questioning the good faith of the company. The advertisement reported the findings of the lung specialist and ended with an appeal for solving the health problems in the plant through collective bargaining.

Management's response was to insist that conditions weren't as bad as charged, that not as many workers had silicosis as reported by the doctor, and that improvements were already being made. The foundry took advantage of the anticommunist hysteria then engulfing the country to further claim that the union's interest in pursuing the silicosis problem was a calculated effort to divert attention from recent congressional hearings in Schenectady. Those hearings had been set up by an antilabor congressional committee with the aim of undermining the confidence of UE members in their union by making its activities appear to be part of a communist conspiracy.

The union's demands for improved conditions in the foundry dated from a full six months before the congressional committee even appeared on the scene. The company's decision to drag the "red" issue into the dispute was viewed by the workers as a transparent attempt to divert public attention from their dangerous environmental conditions. Union pressure within the plant and demand from the community where the workers lived eventually resulted in major plant improvements.[60]

Commercial media often reported on labor strikes but rarely reported union efforts to protect the lives and health of working people. On the other hand, protection of workers' health was always a concern of union publications like *UE News*. Introduction of fluorescent lamps into factories soon after World War II presented UE with yet another serious health hazard to address. A substance called beryllium was used to coat fluorescent glass tubes that give the lamps their glow. If a lamp broke, a worker came in direct contact with poisonous chemicals. State health authorities in New Jersey diagnosed the deaths of several workers as beryllium poisoning. A number of deaths were similarly ascribed to beryllium at a Sylvania plant in Salem, Massachusetts.

At the 1947 UE convention in Boston, Dr. Harriet L. Hardy of the State Labor Department had met with delegates from the lamp plants covered by UE contracts. She noted that doctors found it difficult to diagnose beryllium poisoning because of symptoms similar to pneumonia and other respiratory diseases, and the number of reported cases tended therefore to underestimate factory fatalities. Some victims did not get sick until as many as six years after exposure. While companies maintained there was no other way to manufacture the lamps, the union insisted there had to be a way of producing the lamps without such a lethal poison.

The manufacture of fluorescent fixtures later created a similar problem for workers at GE plants in Hudson Falls and Fort Edwards, New York. In 1969, workers began to report sickness from the use of epoxy glues. A terse note from Local 332 went to GE management: "The next job using epoxy, unions will file grievance." Seeking help to publicize the complaint, the local union sent me the label on the material they believed was causing the problem. The red, white and blue label read

> ***Danger:*** Causes severe eye and skin burns. Do not get in eyes, on skin, on clothing.... Avoid breathing or exposure to vapor. In case of contact immediately flush skin or eyes with plenty of water for at least 15 minutes; for eyes, get prompt medical attention. Remove contaminated clothing, including shoes, wash clothing before reuse, discard contaminated shoes.

After the union gathered a large amount of factual evidence, it brought the New York State Labor Department into an investigation of the hazardous conditions. It eventually became evident that users of the lamps at home were also at risk and the use of beryllium was finally banned. Only through union pressure and consumer health problems, did the company finally eliminate the most dangerous conditions in the factory.

The electric companies always kept a close watch on union actions and the *UE News* reports that called for an end to toxic materials and workplace hazards. Several days after *UE News* reported that 11 men were carried off their jobs because of unbearable heat in the machine department at the GE clock factory in Ashland, Massachusetts, I received an angry letter from a manager. He accused me of running a story that was "totally untrue and in our opinion represents irresponsible reporting of a nature that could damage the Ashland plant's reputation." (August 17, 1971).

UE News never printed a story dealing with plant conditions without carefully checking facts, not only with local union officers but also with national union staff responsible for the particular company involved. Our staff responsible for union relations with GE and Westinghouse were stationed in the national UE office because of countrywide significance of union agreements with those companies. As a journalist in the national union headquarters, I had direct access to information about conditions in local factories and so I had complete confidence in the accuracy of the Ashland report.

After the passage of the *Occupational Safety and Health Act* in 1970, the union added a health and safety medical expert to its staff. He not only handled requests from local unions but also initiated programs to address potential hazardous conditions in factories. He also began to write a regular column on health and safety that became a permanent feature of *UE News.*

Two New York State General Electric plants that had previously been identified with health problems related to epoxy again landed on newspaper front pages because of their use of polychlorinated biphenyls (PCBs). PCBs were known to cause severe skin and liver problems. In Japan, PCBs accidentally leaked into commercial cooking oil with devastating health consequences. The incident was widely reported in the United States. In 1975, the New York State Environmental Protection Agency began an investigation into the reported discharge of PCBs into the Hudson River in New York.

At GE and other companies, PCBs were used to insulate transformers. Estimates of the quantity of PCBs poured into the 315 miles along the Hudson River ran into hundreds of thousands of pounds. The state investigation found that Hudson River fish were absorbing PCBs in fat. This was so dangerous to the health of anyone eating the fish that the State Health Department recommended that no person should eat more than half a pound of striped bass a month. Eventually the state banned all fishing in the Hudson. In 1987, the Department estimated that it might take three decades before levels of PCBs in striped bass in the Hudson would drop to an amount acceptable to the Federal Food and Drug Administration.

A detailed program by UE on how to end PCB hazards inside electric plants contributed to public demand for a substitute for PCBs. *UE News* was able to report (December 20, 1976) that the Monsanto Chemical Company, sole U.S. manufacturer of PCBs, had agreed to halt PCB production by the spring of 1977, and to adopt substitute products in its U.S. plants by that date.

Pensions

Stories about retirement were among the most difficult I covered over the years. Loss of a regular paycheck made a huge cut in workers' incomes and they also faced medical problems not covered by insurance. Despite UE's efforts to bargain over retirement issues, company officials stubbornly sought to deny unions the right to speak for retired workers.

In 1948, a federal government survey found that the minimum income needed by an elderly couple was $140 a month while another study done by the University of California set $220 a month as an "adequate" standard. Meanwhile, the average monthly GE pension was $32, while the average Social Security received by an elderly couple came to $40. People who worked hard all their lives were retiring straight into poverty.

Even though major corporations steadfastly sought to deny UE the right to represent retired workers, no contract negotiations went by without UE bringing up the subject of pensions. The union also made successful efforts to publicize the mean-spirited stance of the corporations toward retirement. *UE News* continuously reported the status of retired workers and local unions and then took this information to their communities. The union stepped up its campaign to establish $125 monthly pensions in its 1948 negotiations with major corporations.

In furtherance of the union's retirement efforts, I interviewed retired workers in places where they lived, including Springfield, Massachusetts, where three years earlier I had gone to report on the strike against Westinghouse. One retiree, at age 80, had received an engraved citation from the U.S. Army for his valuable service in World War II. Now, at 83 years old, he was getting a monthly pension check from Westinghouse for $9. 99. "Down at the bank they ask me," he said, "what's the matter with Westinghouse, can't they afford the extra penny?"

Everyone's personal story added to the accumulating picture of hardship and bitterness. As *UE News* coverage of the pension campaign continued, many retired workers began sending more stories and information. That's how we happened to get a copy of a letter sent by Westinghouse Vice President Ralph Stewart to a retiring worker in May 1946. It read: "Naturally we are sorry to lose the services of so old and valuable an employee but I am sure that you are looking forward to a well-earned rest and the new leisure which your retirement will bring." It had the look of a form letter that went to every worker approaching compulsory retirement.

The speciousness of the whole thing was summed up in the next sentence: "According to our annuity records, you will receive a Lump Sum Settlement of $75. 02." The letter went on to advise on how to apply for unemployment compensation benefits. After his retirement, the employee who sent us the letter worked at a menial job to make a subsistence living.

Meanwhile, GE was proclaiming to the world that "progress is our most important product." However, when it came to retired employees in comparison to Westinghouse's extremely low pensions, GE offered no pension at all. They abolished their pension system as soon as Social Security came into being in 1935.

Thirteen years later, in 1948, an historic event took place when a group of elderly men walked into a meeting where contract negotiations with GE were in session. This action was arranged by UE to bypass the company's insistence that the union was not authorized to speak for retired workers. Weighing the possible bad publicity of ejecting the intruders, GE officials decided to go forward with negotiations. It was the very first time that representatives of the company ever sat in the same room with retired workers and listened to their demands.

GE finally established a pension plan in 1950. It was nowhere near what was minimally needed, but it was the beginning. An internal corporate document obtained by the union showed that failure to establish an inclusive pension plan was hurting the company through high worker turnover. The memo stated: "Some of our people no doubt interpreted the discontinuance of our former pension plans as a change in company attitude toward our employees' general welfare."

I continued to maintain a strong interest in covering retirement issues through my column in *UE News*. I closely followed one of the most effective organizations of retired GE employees at the company's locomotive plant in Erie, Pennsylvania in the early 1960s. In their working years they were active in the union and had a lot of accumulated organizational experience. The Erie plant employed more than 6000 workers who were contributing to the city's economy. In 1963, the company reported that 1,180 of its former employees were drawing pensions. While such pensions had obviously made some improvement in people's lives in comparison to when the union first pressured the company into establishing a pension plan, the actual amount of the pension still left former workers at a poverty level.

Several months after GE made its report on pensions, I visited Erie to interview retired workers for *UE News*. While I was there, the U.S. Labor Department declared Erie to be a "depressed area." Vacant stores visibly lined its main streets. The most recent government cost of living figures estimated that a retired couple over sixty-five would need $3,102 a year to provide for "no more than basic essentials of consumption" in Western Pennsylvania. None of the retired workers I interviewed came anywhere near getting the basic subsistence amount cited in the report. In addition, living costs had already risen substantially since that report was released. The union made it an important part of its bargaining drive to inform the Erie community that raising the purchasing ability of retirees would also help restore the city's economic health.

The union continued to make the needs of retired workers an essential part of its bargaining program. It vigorously protested when companies began cutting pensions whenever Social Security benefits rose. This type of offset became a common practice at Westinghouse, GE and other corporations. Bitter complaints from union members about the offsets reached local and national union offices. According to union estimates, had GE not cut pensions by the amount Social Security was raised in 1963, its $150 million after-tax-profit for the previous year would have been reduced by only $45,000. Like Sisyphus in Greek mythology who was condemned to push a huge stone up a hill only to have it roll down again as he neared the top, retired workers at that time were being condemned to pension cuts with every increase in Social Security. The union never ceased making the needs of retired workers an essential part of its bargaining program.

Many changes were taking place in my personal life. During the 1960s, our children Richard and Betty both graduated from the University of Wisconsin in Madison, where I had so reluctantly dropped out of school during the Depression. Betty later became an elementary school teacher in Manhattan and won awards for her excellence as an educator. Richard earned his doctorate in Social Anthropology at the University of California at Berkeley and developed an expertise on agricultural cooperatives in

India. Having settled in California, he subsequently had a career implementing federal laws on environmental and historical protection.

After my children went off to college, I enrolled in classes at the Brooklyn Botanical Garden for growing tropical indoor plants and began seriously growing bromeliads and orchids on our sun porch overlooking East 5th Street. I brought back some of these plants from travel over the years and never stopped deriving great joy from this year-round exotic garden. I continued to grow tomatoes every summer in our small back yard. After I started to raise these tomatoes I was never able to eat any other tomatoes, even in the off-season. I also happily got away from the pressures of work and world events by building furniture in the attic.

CHAPTER TWENTY

Cold War Trade

In the early 1970s, an economic depression caused the machine tool sector of American industry to be working at less than half capacity. The consequences for highly skilled workers who made machines that make other machines was devastating. Many UE members worked in Vermont, a state that prided itself on being the "cradle of the American machine tool industry."

Political decisions made in Washington were intensifying this industrywide depression. The Union was offering to fulfill work on purchase orders to U.S. manufacturers estimated at close to a billion dollars in total value. Representatives of Soviet industry were enthusiastically visiting U.S. plants, including those represented by UE, seeking to buy machine tools. American manufacturers had also been going to Moscow looking for business orders. They even set up trade shows there to promote their products, all to no avail because Cold War policies emerging in Washington prohibited manufacturers from accepting orders from the Soviet Union.

UE leaders President Albert J. Fitzgerald, Secretary-Treasurer James J. Matles and Hugh Harley, Director of Organization, initiated a union campaign to end the senseless economic blockade. They asked me to use *UE News* to help union members in Vermont in their efforts to get Washington to allow Soviet purchases of American equipment. I studied industry publications, talked to officers of the manufacturers' association and interviewed officials of corporations with which the union had collective bargaining agreements.

The union found that an acrimonious battle was going on within the Nixon Administration over the issue of whether to trade with the Soviet Union. Among the protagonists were Commerce Secretary Maurice H. Stans, who favored letting American industry sell to the Soviet Union, and Henry A. Kissinger, the President's national security adviser, who was determined not to permit such trade. Stans had met with top Soviet officials and foresaw that trade with the USSR could reach billions of dollars. The President, according to press reports, was at that time leaning toward Kissinger and his ally, Defense Secretary Melvin R. Laird. Each of these men had his own reasons for standing in the way of trade. Kissinger wanted to force the Soviet Union to accept certain unrelated political conditions. Laird, speaking for the military, raised the possibility that the Russians would buy American machinery to build equipment for use against U.S. interests in the Vietnam War. The White House changed its position back and forth several times. For the union to plunge into this morass looked nearly hopeless, especially since McCarthyism was still pervasive in its adverse affects on the labor movement.

As an observer at some union meetings where officials were present from four companies holding UE collective bargaining agreements, I tried to figure out how these manufacturers stood on the military's reasons for barring Soviet trade and how much American business was really at stake.

President John E. Barbier of the Fellows Gear Shaper plant in Springfield, Vermont, claimed that at least 98 percent of the products made at his plant were also available in other countries, so the Soviets could easily acquire them from our competitors. He expressed a strong belief that U.S. industry should be allowed to compete on even terms in the international market. According to my notes from the meeting, he complained that "Japan and the rest have had a bonanza.... You beat your brains out, get to Russia, get the contract, and then you come back and the U.S. Commerce Department won't give you a license."

As Vice President of the National Machine Tool Builders Association, Barbier spoke for an important sector of American industry. His view of the situation was shared by other corporate officials, including R. S. Jones, vice-president and general manager of Jones & Lamson, then a leading machine tool manufacturer. He told me there were numerically controlled lathes being shipped to Russia from Sweden that were similar to his company's product. Jones mentioned something I had already become aware of during the 1930's Depression. His company and other machine tool makers were sustained at that time in large measure by Soviet orders.

It was especially galling to learn from corporate officials that even some of their patents were being sub-licensed to foreign firms. An example was the Pneumodynamics Corporation in Windsor, Vermont, which had licensed a company in England to produce its product, the Fellows Gear Shaper, under the name "Fellows-England." Employers overseas were thus making profits from U.S. patents and workers outside the U.S. were getting American jobs.

Unlike a large city where poverty and decay are often visible, a visitor passing through the clean, neat town of Springfield would have no idea of the difficulties its citizens were then facing. The office of the Springfield Chamber of Commerce could be found on the square just up the street so I went there for information on the area's history. One of the booklets proclaimed the town "*The Cradle of Invention*" with special reference to the manufacture of machinery dating back to 1829 when the Parks & Woolson textile machinery plant opened. Now workers at the plant represented by UE were among those in desperate need of more orders.

An overall view of the local employment situation emerged at my meeting with the town's director of employment services. He held a list of over 1,600 people looking for work when there were only 80 openings. The jobless rate hovered at 15 percent and lines of unemployed workers at this office overflowed onto the street.

From the union office on the banks of the Black River, which flows south to join the Connecticut River, I climbed the low green hills to a quiet residential area where the state's local Social Welfare Department was located. The director gave me figures that showed a sharp increase in their case load within the past year. For some laid-off union members this was the first time they needed unemployment insurance in more than 20 years at the plant.

While the union and employers did not relinquish their traditional adversarial relations on wages and working conditions, UE's offer to help break the Cold War blockade seemed to bring a welcome truce. The union brought the entire community into this campaign for jobs. Members distributed a leaflet headed: "You Can Help Bring Back Jobs to Vermont," which informed the community that Soviet orders were going to foreign companies. *UE News* hit hard on this issue, asking people to write their representatives in Washington and organize in support of union demands.

The community's response and the letters that came back to the union from Washington were generally favorable. Only one New Hampshire legislator expressed opposition to the union's cause. Republican Representative James C. Cleveland stated that until the Vietnam War was over we should not trade with the Russians who were supporting North Vietnam: "I am sure none of your members would want to indirectly assist either in the killing of Americans or in the weakening of our efforts to negotiate with the Russians." Just six months later, this same congressman's office had turned around and replied favorably to a union request for assistance in obtaining a government export license for more than 150 machine tools built by the Bryant Grinder Company.

UE decided to take the fight to Washington and persuade President Richard Nixon and the Pentagon to lift the blockade. UE President Fitzgerald headed a delegation that included Paul Seymour, president of the union's New England district, and James Kane, president of the Springfield local, who was employed at the Jones & Lamson plant. I had the opportunity to accompany them to meetings with government officials. My previous visits to the Pentagon had been to participate in peace demonstrations. As I plodded through the endless halls of the immense Pentagon structure, I was fully aware that I was in the center of the military-industrial complex from which the Vietnam War was being directed.

At the U.S. State and Commerce departments, our delegation generally experienced approval for our efforts. Republican George Aiken of Vermont arranged for us to see officials at the Pentagon, including the Deputy Assistant Secretary in charge of war production and material acquisition. Military officials came to the meeting, including General Charles

Fletcher and Howard Millbourn, the Pentagon assistant with expertise on machine tools. As members of the union delegation described the extent of the machine industry's unemployment problems, General Fletcher began reciting the Pentagon's theories about the danger of supplying machinery to the Soviet Union. Our group was ready with specific examples of American and European companies that were going ahead and filling Soviet orders from their overseas plants. "That's right, that's what's happening," the Pentagon's expert on machine tools interjected, apparently supporting our position. Then the General precipitously announced that the positions of the President and State Department "overruled" any other advise on the issue. That brought the meeting to an abrupt end.

At this unexpected development, our union delegation went straight to see Senator Aiken, but we were unable to make further progress in seeing Washington leaders with influence over trade issues of concern to the union. The senator informed our delegation that some U.S. corporations were actually using government opposition to trade with the Soviet Union to their own competitive advantage. He mentioned the recent campaign by a nationally-known company to prevent one of its U.S. competitors from accepting an order to build a plant in the Soviet Union. They had even gone so far as to enlist a national veterans' organization to help them block the order scheduled for construction of the plant. The company then turned around and grabbed the order for itself.

While it was UE that initiated the difficult effort to turn around a Republican Administration, the UAW joined the effort a year later. A statement adopted by that union's executive board in July 1972 pointed out that in 1969 European companies sent $296 million worth of machine tools into the Soviet Union compared with the U.S. total of $18 million. The statement called this "suicidal" for the U.S. economy.

Later in 1972, *The Washington Post* featured a front-page story headed "U.S. in a Policy Shift, Widens Soviet Trade." The article made special mention of the "depressed state of the American machine tool industry." This change in policy that UE had so vigorously supported soon brought visible gains to workers in the machine tool industry across the country.

A second reason for my trips to Springfield in the early 1970s was to assist a Soviet television crew. They were documenting the effects their country's trade was having on a local American community. It made for a rare sight on the main street of the New England town when correspondents for Izvestia and Moscow radio and TV stations interviewed passersby. The visitors set up their cameras and recording equipment for an interview in their native language at a Ukrainian-born worker's home. There was an interesting moment in this unusual visit when an attempt was made to translate "factory troubleshooter" into Russian.

In 1978, UE invited a delegation of the Soviet Union's power and electrical workers union to visit the United States. At a welcoming gathering at UE national headquarters in New York City, union President Fitzgerald pointed out how this was the first group of Soviet trade unionists granted permission to enter our country since the beginning of the Cold War in the late 1940s. Getting permission for this group to enter the United States had not come easily. The day before the delegation was to leave Moscow, UE officers received a cablegram from the Soviet Electrical Workers Union saying their delegates were denied visas at the American embassy. A union friend in Congress helped persuade the State Department to make the visas available the next day even though it was a Saturday. At 3:00 a.m. New York time and already morning in Moscow, I called the offices of the trade union there and directed the delegation to go immediately to the U.S. embassy to pick up their visas.

The Russian group that showed up for the ten-day trip to New England and Pennsylvania included the president of the power and electrical workers union; the president of the Irkutsk, Siberia, branch where members worked at huge hydroelectric power stations; a lathe operator at a Sverdlovsk transformer and generator plant in the Ural Mountains; the head of the union committee at a Moscow lamp factory; and an interpreter. The union president was a tall, broad-shouldered man whose good humor and lack of bureaucratic pretense had previously made him an appreciated host for a UE delegation that visited the Soviet Union in 1972. During that trip we took to referring to him as "Program," the word he often used to remind everyone of our schedule.

I drove with the Russian visitors by station wagon to Vermont to see the factories that made equipment for Soviet factories and to meet union members there. A display of American and Soviet flags met us as we entered the Bryant factory. A glass case on a wall contained a company catalogue in Russian dating back to 1934. In that year, President Roosevelt finally recognized the existence of the Soviet government that had been established 17 years before, during the Russian revolution. This display and the flags served as a reminder of how U.S. trade with the Soviet Union constantly depended on political relations between the two countries.

The union delegation from Russia was the last one to visit the United States for a long time. Within a few months, an amendment tacked onto a military appropriations bill gave the State Department authority to ban any trade union delegation that it thought included communists. It was a restriction that AFL-CIO President George Meany strongly promoted at the time and it was strictly enforced in the decade to follow. The ban included countries such as Italy and France where communists were in the leadership of the largest labor organizations. The infamous "noncommunist" test in the *Taft-Hartley Act* that the Supreme Court had found unconstitutional was now given new life through this application to foreign visitors.

The success of sensible trading policies with the Soviet Union that benefited American workers unfortunately turned out to be just a fleeting armistice in a continuing war. By the end of the 1970's, restrictions on Soviet trade were reinstated by Democratic President Jimmy Carter and continued by Republican President Ronald Reagan. Unemployment again hit the American machine tool industry and the rest of U.S. basic industry. A *New York Times* story (January 16, 1987) reported that while Defense Secretary Caspar Weinberger was working to prevent the export of equipment from the U.S. to the Soviet Union for production of oil and gas, the U.S. State and Commerce Departments were publishing the fact that America's Japanese and European allies were supplying them such equipment. Ironically, these government reports actually noted that the trade controls were more damaging to American business than to the Soviet Union.

Unfortunately, the surge in the machine tool industry was not successful in the long term. Early in 1988, James Kane, who returned to Springfield, Vermont, after retiring as UE president, informed me that barely 30 people were working at the Jones & Lamson plant that had employed over 700 people when he worked there two decades before. In Windsor, Vermont, the Cone plant was struggling to stay afloat. This plant, which for a long time had been assigning Soviet orders to its British affiliate, was trying to involve the local union in a joint ownership plan. The record of such efforts at other companies had not been good, and UE always opposed such plans without exception when they were brought up by union locals. Even up north at Fairbanks, Vermont, where townspeople and workers had at one time successfully raised funds to keep the company from deserting the state, unemployment was now very high. The state was no longer the "cradle of the American machine tool industry." It was now becoming its graveyard.

CHAPTER TWENTY-ONE

Vietnam Is Union Business

Delegates were initially encouraged when President Lyndon Johnson made a campaign pledge at the Democratic National Convention in fall 1964 not to send American boys to fight in Vietnam. This pledge barely outlasted the November vote count. Opposition to the war soon became equated with unpatriotic support for North Vietnam and promotion of communism. That same year, despite some strong opposition, delegates at the annual UE convention approved a resolution announcing its opposition to U.S. military involvement in the Vietnam conflict.

Opposition to the war at that time was based largely on college campuses. However, with the growth of the antiwar movement, the specter of McCarthyism again loomed up within the labor movement, with AFL-CIO President George Meany leading the charge. Meany lost no time in denouncing academics as "victims of communist propaganda." (*AFL-CIO News*, May 3, 1965). For UE, which was still struggling to overcome its losses from the splits in the labor movement caused by the McCarthy hearings in the 1950s, even taking a mild position against the war brought risks.

At factory gates where UE representatives attempted to bring unorganized workers the message of unionism, they were still confronted by organizers from other unions who used the anticommunist shibboleth to undercut UE's union-building efforts. The four other major unions competing for membership in the industries where UE was active all committed themselves to supporting the war. Even UAW President Walter Reuther, regarded by many as representing a more liberal section of the AFL-CIO than Meany on most issues, told his union's membership that if the United States pulled out of Vietnam there would be a "chain reaction and no small country in South Asia would be secure against subversion, infiltration and communist penetration." (*AFL-CIO News*, December 18, 1965). However, many rank and file UAW members held views against the war and eventually made their voices heard.

Some union leaders berated their members who joined antiwar protests. Officers of the United Steelworkers Union warned that "our people who protest against this country's policies are in effect encouraging continuation of the war and discouraging settlement by negotiation." (October 30, 1965). The Machinists Union paper featured a statement by President Johnson claiming that the security of the United States would be imperiled if the U.S. was driven out of Vietnam. The Defense Department later financed a trip to the war front by representatives of the paper. After returning from Vietnam, the paper ran a two-page photo-spread entitled "How U.S. Air Power Is Wrecking Red Timetable in Vietnam," with pictures and captions supplied by the Pentagon.

The IUE, which had been set up to undermine and replace UE in 1949, at first endorsed Meany's pro-war policy but later dropped the issue entirely. In its publications between 1965 and 1971, there were only two references to the war. One was an announcement in December 1965 that the union would accept contributions from the members to help set up a refugee camp in South Vietnam. The other was an item ridiculing a UE resolution passed by members that expressed their opposition to the war.

At every UE convention during the Vietnam War, members continued to pass resolutions against U.S. military involvement. These resolutions opposed the war for both moral and economic reasons. National officers and local delegates fought hard to pass these resolutions in the face of resistance from some members who wanted to limit the union's position to simply supporting the troops. The top leadership of most UE local unions remained in support of the war. However, opposition to the war continued to grow among rank and file members.

Three years after the first UE peace resolution in 1964, leaders of 14 national AFL-CIO affiliates invited UE to join them in sponsoring a National Labor Assembly for Peace in Chicago that took place on

November 11–12, 1967. This meeting was held on the anniversary of the armistice that ended the First World War. I attended the Chicago meeting as a reporter for *UE News* and was elated to find that UE finally had significant antiwar allies within the broader labor movement. We had first supported peace at a time when taking an antiwar position was daring and unpopular, and when its only labor allies came from a few unions that survived when the CIO expelled eleven unions for supposed communist influence in 1949.

The Reverend Martin Luther King, Jr. addressed the Chicago peace meeting on the labor movement's longstanding failure to take a stand on the war. "The absence of the voice of labor," he told 500 delegates present at the University of Chicago, "has been all the more tragic because it may be the decisive voice in tipping the scales of peace." At the same meeting, Harvard economics Professor John Kenneth Galbraith traced U.S. involvement in the war back to the anticommunism hysteria of the 1950s. He characterized the war as one of resistance by the Vietnamese people to colonialism.

AFL-CIO President George Meany continued to condemn the labor leaders who had defied him by breaking away from his pro-war position. He extended his support for the war to the length of refusing to endorse the pro-labor Democratic Party candidate for president in 1968, North Dakota Senator George McGovern, because of his opposition to the war. Meany had thereby helped elect an antilabor candidate, Richard Nixon. Although Nixon eventually campaigned for president in 1968 with a pledge to get out of the war, like Presidents Eisenhower, Kennedy, and Johnson before him, he ended up expanding the conflict.

Many senators and representatives, including William Fulbright, Albert Gore, Morris Udall, and Robert Kennedy, began reversing their positions on the war. How many of these turnabouts were due to recognition of the real nature of the war, or pressure from the rising popular opposition to the war was impossible to tell. Meanwhile, UE had a principled record of analyzing the true facts of the war and opposing it from the start.

When the Ohio National Guard killed four students at an antiwar demonstration at Kent State University in May 1970, even stronger labor opposition to the war began to develop. UE's General Executive Board called the killings of the four students who were engaged in a peaceful protest "a tragic product of an administration in Washington which has made escalation of war abroad and repression at home its most distinguishing characteristics." *UE News* and union leaders continued to urge our members to demand that President Nixon take America out of the war.

By summer 1972, close to 46,000 Americans had died in the war as well as an estimated 2,000,000 south Asians. At the headquarters of the Teamsters Union in St. Louis in June, 1972, more than 1,000 delegates from 35 international unions, including UE and its president, Albert J. Fitzgerald, finally met and formed a broad-based labor effort to promote an end to the war.

By 1973, the U.S. death toll had surpassed 55,000 people. Huge demonstrations across the country and at the very doors of the Pentagon made continuation of the hostilities nearly impossible. It still took more than a year for AFL-CIO President George Meany to accomplish his personal "withdrawal" through an interview on Dick Cavett's nationally televised show. He stated he would not have supported the war if he had "known then what I know now." (December 1974). Let be said that it wasn't just ignorance of facts about the war that led Meany to support the war for so long, but rather his unwavering dedication to the cause of fighting communism. This personal crusade prevented him from ever seeing the realities of the war.

There were few pieces I was called on to write in my many years with *UE News* that gave me as much satisfaction as a full-page summary in spring 1975, recounting the history of U.S. intervention in Southeast Asia and UE's longstanding opposition to the war. Five American presidents entangled the American people in the Vietnam morass. The last one, Gerald Ford, took over as president after the Watergate scandal drove Richard Nixon from office. Ford could no longer convince Congress to finance the U.S. bombings of Vietnam, Laos and Cambodia. The *Case-Church Amendment* effectively ended military participation in the war by prohibiting use of American funds for direct military activity by U.S. forces after August 1973. At last, the American people had prevailed.

It is fitting that I have ended this account with a chapter on the Vietnam War. Early in this book I described my experiences as a leader in the antiwar and antifascist movements prior to the Second World War. Now I have come full-circle to my work with UE and its opposition to the war. I wanted to record UE's singular efforts in the 1960s to influence an end to the Vietnam War. I also wished to bring home the fact that working people and labor unions, as crucial players in this nation's economy and culture, must have a full voice in its international policies, in war and in peace.

Notes

1 On September 7, 1917, the government of President Woodrow Wilson responded by conducting simultaneous raids on the headquarters of the Socialist Party and the IWW all across the country. The Party's entire executive committee was then indicted under the espionage law, and dozens of labor and socialist newspapers were suppressed. Rose Pastor Stokes, a socialist, was punished with a ten-year prison sentence for writing a letter to a newspaper opposing the war. Other opponents of war who were arrested by federal agents included pacifists, anarchists, conscientious objectors, Quakers, Mennonites, and Irish *Sinn Feiners*. In a single month, 2000 members of IWW were waiting trial for speaking out against the war with many defendants getting heavy fines and prison sentences of up to ten or 20 years.

2 For making an antiwar speech at Canton, Ohio, on June 16, 1918, Eugene V. Debs, the Socialist Party leader and four-time presidential candidate, was sentenced to ten years in federal prison. His appeal was rejected by the unanimous vote of the Supreme Court, including that of the liberal justice Oliver Wendell Holmes. Debs entered the federal prison at Moundsville, West Virginia, on April 13, 1919, five months after the war's end, and was transferred to the Atlanta penitentiary two months later. In response to a nationwide petition campaign, Republican President Warren G. Harding pardoned the 63-year-old Debs on Christmas Day, 1921. While in prison, Debs drew 920,000 votes as his party's 1920 presidential candidate.

3 One of the many achievements of the traditional pacifist organizations took place in February 1932 at the League of Nations World Disarmament Conference. They submitted disarmament petitions signed by 80 million people, including half a million Americans. After five months of unproductive diplomatic haggling, the League of Nations Disarmament Conference shut down at the end of June 1932.

4 At the conclusion of the Amsterdam meeting, the delegate from WILPF reported that 2,244 delegates had attended from 57 countries. Of these, she noted: "1,856 were workers, 129 intellectuals, 72 peasants, and 67 women." (*Rosika Schwimmer Peace Collection* at the New York Public Library).

5 Religious leaders who attended the congress included Rabbi Barnett Brickner, Cleveland; Reverend William Lloyd Imes of the St. James Presbyterian Church in New York; Rabbi Elias Margolies, president of the Synagogue Council of America, Baltimore; Rabbi Edward Israel; Rev. Francis C.

Schlater, United Minister's Council; and William Spofford, executive secretary of the Church League for Industrial Democracy.

6 At times, special appeals were made to a selected group of the organization's backers, specifically for the purpose of developing the peace movement among young people. Those who responded to these appeals included Professor Robert Morss Lovett, an eminent professor of English at the University of Chicago, whose *British Prose and Verse* was a standard text in college courses across the country; and William Spofford, editor of *The Witness*, a publication of the Episcopal Church.

7 Reports of successful branch organizing came from all over the country. Branches even included World War I veterans, fraternal organizations and Temple Sisterhoods in suburban New York. Reports came from Kansas; New Orleans; Springfield, Massachusetts; Seattle; Philadelphia; Dagmar, Montana; and Toledo, Ohio, where 49 organizations formed a chapter. At a Wisconsin state conference, among over 217 delegates in attendance, 68 delegates came from unions of the American Federation of Labor who committed themselves to building the League. Branches were also formed in Perth Amboy and Newark, New Jersey; Hartford and New Haven, Connecticut; Kalamazoo and Detroit, Michigan; Milwaukee; Boston; Youngstown, Ohio; Chicago; and Erie, Pennsylvania. Requests for help in setting up local committees also came from Eugene, Oregon; Elbow Lake, Minnesota; Hager City and Superior, Wisconsin; Wilkes Barre, Pennsylvania; Sioux City, Iowa; Aberdeen, South Dakota; Pueblo, Colorado; Little Rock, Arkansas; Jacksonville, Florida; Louisville, Kentucky; Grand Rapids, Michigan; Butte, Montana; and Wheeling, West Virginia. Farmers in Nebraska, Michigan, and Idaho also formed branches.

8 Much of the information in this book about League activities on the West Coast was researched at the Bancroft Library in Berkeley. Especially valuable were their collections of *The Western Worker* and *Pacific Weekly* newspapers from the 1930's. Matt Crawford, a leader in California cooperative organizations, and Clifton Amsbury, member of the Abraham Lincoln Brigade, provided me with first-hand information on the West Coast peace movement during oral interviews.

9 In 1936, western locals of ILA seceded and became the International Longshore and Warehouse Union (ILWU), affiliated with the CIO.

10 In response to an American Legion march in Oakland, California, on Armistice Day, 1935, the League organized a large antiwar meeting. It was held at the Oakland Civic Auditorium and endorsed by the Alameda County Central Labor Council.

11 A follow-up meeting to the San Francisco meetings in April, 1935, was held by the Northern California District Conference Against War and Fascism on December 14 and 15, 1935. Related to this meeting, *The Pacific Weekly* dated December 9, 1935, published the following: "Although only two years old, the American League Against War and Fascism already represents more than 2,500,000 people who are either members of the League or affiliate organizations. Following are the aims and objectives of the League:

> 1. The League works toward the stopping of the manufacture and transportation of munitions and all other materials essential to the conduct of war.
>
> 2. It exposes the extensive preparations for war and works toward the transfer of the war funds to the rehabilitation of the unemployed.
>
> 3. It forms committees of action in every important center and industry to defend the civil liberties of minority groups and so stop the growth of the fascist trends of industry and government.
>
> 4. It enlists the youth, especially those who by the crisis have been deprived of training in industries and are therefore more susceptible to fascist and war propaganda.
>
> 5. It seeks the support for this program of all organizations and individuals interested in the prevention of war — paying special attention to labor, veteran, unemployed, and farmer organizations.
>
> 6. It conducts educational programs against war and fascism, to unite all forces in common resistance to these allied destroyers of mankind.

12 Other well-known artists who contributed to *Fight* were Louis Lozowick, Syd Hoff, Ad Reinhardt, Peggy Bacon, William Gropper, Hugo Gellert, Anton Refregier, John Groth, Lynd Ward and Wanda Gag. Refregier's murals depicting incidents in San Francisco's history, including persecution of Chinese people in California, the Tom Mooney case, and the 1934 general strike, grace the walls of the San Francisco's Rincon Annex Post Office. This mural was one of the many art works made possible by Depression-era federal programs.

13 The League's commitment to including news about the labor movement in the magazine led Joseph Pass to solicit articles from trade union leaders.

Among those who wrote for *Fight* were United Mine Workers' leader John L. Lewis, founding president of the CIO; A.F. Whitney, president of the Brotherhood of Railway Trainmen; Heywood Broun, noted newspaper columnist and founding president of the American Newspaper Guild; and Reid Robinson, president of the Mine, Mill, and Smelter Workers. A reader could find in a single issue views from a worker, professor, clergyman, internationally known refugees from Germany, and an article about California farmers.

14 Among those in the delegation to Washington were Dorothy Detzer of the WILPF; Mary Fox, executive secretary of the League for Industrial Democracy; and Maxwell Stewart of the Foreign Policy Association. Like Matthews, Stewart was one of the Socialist leaders who refused to break with the League when the Socialist Party withdrew in summer 1933. The delegation also included Charles Zimmerman of the AFL's International Ladies Garment Workers Union; Monroe Sweetland of the Socialist-led Intercollegiate League for Industrial Democracy (the student section of the League for Industrial Democracy); Clarence Hathaway of the Communist Party; Communist labor organizer Ella Reeve Bloor, usually referred to as "Mother Bloor," and three representatives of the League's Youth Section, including myself.

15 Navy Secretary Claude A. Swanson stated that it was government policy to build a navy second-to-none, "to support ... especially the development of American foreign commerce." *Fight* reported (January 1934) that of the total appropriated for public works to relieve unemployment, $585 million was diverted to projects for the army and navy.

16 At that time, Chairman Matthews' wife also left her post as circulation manager for *Fight*. We were never able to pinpoint whether her departure was due to one of the political rifts between the socialists and the communists or to the rumor that her husband was having an affair with an associate of the Socialist Party.

17 Ironically, after leaving the League under the shadow of being an alleged strike-breaker, Matthews expressed his hope that "the work of the League may grow in effectiveness day by day as it confronts the deepening crisis of the world situation. Nothing can ever cause me to forget or to cease to appreciate the part which I had in the formation of the League or the value of the personal associations with its loyal workers...."

18 The books Ward had written previous to assuming the League's chairmanship included *In Place of Profit*, based on a 1931-1932 sabbatical year he spent in the Soviet Union. The book was translated into Chinese and widely distributed. In China, interest in his views apparently was stimulated by a series

of University lectures he delivered several years earlier on the ethical aspects of industrialism and a social interpretation of the Christian gospel. He later undertook his work for the League partly out of a desire to study social incentives that operate successfully without a profit motive. His other books include *Poverty and Wealth* and *The Labor Movement.*

19 Besides Executive Secretary Paul Reid, affectionately called "Tubby" by his fellow seminarians, Ward's other appointments to the League's national leadership included Dr. Margaret Forsyth, an associate of religious education at Columbia University's Teachers College who was a member of the National Board of the YWCA, and Dorothy McConnell, daughter of Methodist Bishop Francis J. McConnell.

20 The more than 200 women who participated in the Women's Commission, led by Margaret Forsyth, were not only concerned about the effects of war and fascism on women. They also made known their objections to "Clause 213A" of the *Federal Economy Act*, which deprived a married woman of a federal civil service job if her husband also held a federal job.

21 At a march of 50,000 Catholic youth who were protesting crime and sex in films in the name of "decency," we distributed a leaflet calling attention to the many films that promoted war. "The machine gun of the gangster kills one, two, ten people," the leaflet claimed, "but the last war killed ten million.... Is it "decent" that millions are starving while $2 billion is spent on war?"

22 Members included Richard Babb Whitten of the Socialist Party of New Orleans; Edith Turner, Indianapolis YWCA; Hayes Beall, national chairman, Methodist Council of Youth; Al Hamilton, Epworth League; Ed Strong, International Negro Youth Movement, Chicago; Gil Green, Young Communist League; representatives of Illinois local unions of the United Mine Workers of America; delegates from the Marine Workers Industrial Union, a precursor to the CIO National Maritime Union; and James A. Wechsler, editor of the Columbia University student paper, *The Daily Spectator.* Wechsler was an active participant in the student antiwar movement at Columbia University and editor of *Erie*, the campus newspaper. Later he became a nationally known journalist. While editor of the New York Post in the 1950s, he was subpoenaed to appear before Senator McCarthy's committee, where he named 59 people as former Young Communist associates. (See *The American Inquisition* by Cedric Belfrage, Bobbs-Merrill, 1973.)

23 The committee of 50 that Swerdloff organized to express the community's opposition to the "goodwill" visit from Hitler's naval emissaries included Thurgood Marshall of the local branch of the NAACP and future Justice of

the United States Supreme court; Samuel Caplan and Angela Bambace of the Ladies Garment Workers Union; I. Keyser, Jewish Building Trades Council; J. Fred Rausch, Baltimore; Eric Jacobs, American Student Union; Ira Berger, International Workers Order; and the Reverend Joseph S. Nowak, Jr.; Swerdloff; and several members of the Johns Hopkins University faculty.

24 Editors' note: In September 1997, the ILWU and other labor supporters picketed the container ship Neptune Jade when it arrived at the Port of Oakland in California. Dockworkers refused to cross picket lines and successfully turned away the ship. It had been loaded in Liverpool, England, by non-union workers after the shipping company fired 500 union workers. After the ship left Oakland, dockworkers in Vancouver and the ports of Yokohama and Kobe, Japan, also refused to unload the vessel.

25 Signers included officers of the Ladies Garment Workers; the United Automobile Workers; the United Textile Workers; the American Federation of Teachers; the Brotherhood of Sleeping Car Porters; Oil Workers Union; Hotel and Restaurant Workers; Mine, Mill and Smelter Workers; United Mine Workers; and the National Radio and Allied Trades National Labor Council. Other signers were Methodist Bishop Francis J. McConnell, Rabbi Stephen S. Wise, and Reverend John Haynes Holmes of New York's Community Church.

26 Carleton Beals, in his book *The Coming Struggle for Latin America* (J. B. Lippincott,1938), characterized information unearthed by the committee's hearings:

> Our American army and navy missions were but sublimated salesmen for American munitions firms. Generals and admirals were on the payrolls of those companies. While our War, Navy and State Departments cooperated in this arming of a continent, the State Department simultaneously was busy talking peace, holding arbitration conferences, trying to settle international disputes and going through all the mumbo jumbo of being interested in the welfare of our neighbors, while actually undermining order and stability.

Beals showed how the same munitions companies were selling both to recognized governments and revolutionaries, and how U.S. military missions in Latin America were teaching police forces how to break strikes and put down political protests.

27 Signs at antiwar rallies often reflected the programs of left-led student organizations: "Strike Against Imperial War;" "Fascism Breeds War;" "Schools

Not Battleships;" and "Abolish the ROTC." ("Battleships or Schools" by Joseph Cohen, National Secretary, National Student League, in *Fight*, April 1935).

28 Even more troubling was Ilma's report of what she had done in Europe, including meetings with Hitler's youth leader, Baldur von Shirach, French fascist leader Bernard de Jouvenal, and Spanish fascist Miguel Primo de Rivera. "It was a thrilling experience to see youth with something to live for," Ilma wrote on her return from Germany. "Whatever else may be said about him, [Hitler] has given them self-respect, courage and new vitality. In contrast, the youth of America are at loose ends and have no ideals, no ambitions, no opportunities...." (*And Now Youth* by Viola Ilma, Robert O. Ballou, New York, 1934.)

29 New York University Professor Harvey Zorbaugh, who did research on Depression-era problems of young people, helped Ilma set up the congress by making available the university's assembly rooms and printing facilities. When he realized the apparent undemocratic nature of the meeting, Zorbaugh undertook to mediate the differences between Ilma and other youth leaders. Two weeks before the scheduled congress, he invited representatives of the twelve organizations to a meeting where he reported to them that Ilma had spurned his efforts. He then announced his withdrawal from the congress.

30 Ilma made another attempt to jump-start her own youth movement at a meeting later held at Rutgers University, but it too fell apart when the delegates again demanded more democratic procedures. Ilma eventually praised the work of the AYC and contradicted attacks on the organization by those who claimed that communists had controlled its founding. Ilma declared in a press release on February 26, 1940 that AYC was "doing a magnificent piece of work which is important to the future of America." (*American Youth Today* by Leslie Gould, Random House, 1940).

31 For a full description of the incident, see the report by Professor Harry C. Steinmetz, representative for the Federated Trades and Labor Council of San Diego, California, in *Pacific Weekly*, August 12, 1935).

32 "On Washington's Birthday, 1937, about four thousand young people joined a pilgrimage to Washington to support passage of this bill. They marched up Pennsylvania Avenue led by a band, carrying huge scrolls bearing one million signatures petitioning for the passage of the *American Youth Act*. Students dressed in cap and gown, farm youth holding hoe and rake, young men in miners' caps, a group of boys dressed in prison suits, and four young Californians

who had crossed the country in a caravan...." (*Youth, the Journal of the Model Congress of the United States*, Milwaukee, Wisconsin, July 2-5, 1937).

33 The *American Youth Act* was later reintroduced in 1938 as S.B. 1463, with nearly six hundred pages of supporting testimony. Although the bill was never enacted, the campaign on its behalf brought to the nation's attention the massive demand for more education and employment opportunities.

34 The petition was signed by the student YWCA and YMCA; the National Student Federation of America; American Youth Congress; Student League for Industrial Democracy; Middle-Atlantic Inter-Seminary Movement; and the Youth Section, American League Against War and Fascism.

35 One of the great values of the annual student strike during the 1930's was that it kept up the ongoing national dialogue about the causes of war. (See *War Our Heritage* by Joseph P. Lash and James A. Wechsler, International Publishers, 1936). Senator Nye and Representative Kvale eventually introduced a bill in Congress in July 1935 to prohibit compulsory military training in high schools and colleges. Although the bill failed to pass, the student movement was learning how to bring its influence on issues of war, education and jobs to high levels of congress.

36 The American delegation of 43 people included American Youth Congress Chairman, William Hinckley; National Student Federation Secretary, Joseph Cadden; Joseph Lash of the American Student Union; Gil Green of the Young Communist League; Myrtle Powell, YWCA; Elizabeth Scott, St. James Presbyterian Church of New York; Harold Peterson, Minnesota Farmer-Labor Party Juniors; Edward Strong, National Negro Congress; and Waldo McNutt and myself representing the Youth Section of the American League Against War and Fascism.

37 In December 1936, the American press reported Loh Tsei's heroism in opposing Japanese aggression against China, and she was referred to as the "Joan of Arc of China" (*New York Herald Tribune*, December 17, 1936). One of the arrested with her was Huang Hua, who later became foreign minister of the People's Republic of China.

38 During a trip to China in 1983, my wife and I met with Lou Tsei in Beijing at the offices of the Council of the Chinese People's Association for Friendship with Foreign Countries. She was a member of its executive board and its All-China Women's Federation. Lu Cui (as her name was now spelled because of orthographic changes in the Chinese language) gave us a copy of an article she wrote in the English language edition of *Women of China* magazine (October 1982). In the article, she credited Edgar Snow for initiating the

international effort to save her and other university students. On the same day we met with her in China, Lu Cui found out she had been elected to the National People's Congress of China.

39 Franco used an army made up largely of mercenaries from Morocco (then a Spanish colony) and received the political and material backing of the Italian and German regimes.

40 The advertisements and greetings also included the YMCA's Association Press; the League for Industrial Democracy; the Socialist Party; Boys' Clubs of America; the Amalgamated Clothing Workers of America and the Communist Party. At the congress, we received greetings from Governor Philip F. LaFollette and Aubrey Williams, executive director of the National Youth Administration, the agency at that time in charge of government programs for young people. Written statements from the Republican Party and Communist Party were read to the gathering. Even President Roosevelt sent a message.

41 Their spokesman, Salvador Garcia, relayed that their primary concerns were racial equality in Cuba, better organization of Cuba's many local youth groups, and replacement of military rule by a civilian government (Milwaukee Journal, July 3, 1937).

42 Following addresses by the national leaders of the Foreign Policy Association, the League of Nations Association, the National Council for Prevention of War, and the American League Against War and Fascism (Dr. Harry F. Ward), the peace committee approved bills condemning fascism in Spain and supporting the Chinese people against Japanese invasion. The peace committee also opposed compulsory military training in America's colleges. The education committee assured young people and teachers that it supported academic freedom. Other committees produced legislation promoting the right of labor to organize freely without being subjected to the kind of terror that resulted in the Memorial Day massacre at Chicago Republic Steel that same year. On that day, ten people died and 30 people were seriously injured after Chicago police shot and clubbed demonstrators.

43 I found valuable information about the student peace movement by doing research at the *Swarthmore College Peace Collection.* A small grant from the Gray Panthers helped finance the travel expenses related to this research.

44 A pamphlet published by the American League Against War and Fascism that year listed as affiliates of this "Christian Front" the following: the Crusaders for Americanism, the American Nationalists, the Christian Mobilizers, the German-American Business League, and the German-American Bund, an

open advocate for Hitler in the United States. The pamphlet was written by Alson J. Smith, minister of the Grace Methodist Church, Waterbury, Connecticut, and secretary of the League's Religious Committee when he wrote the pamphlet.

45 Two years earlier, after leaving the Marines, Butler startled the country by charging before a Congressional committee that a group of wealthy industrialists and bankers had offered him $3 million to lead an American Legion march on Washington. The purpose was to depose President Roosevelt and stage a military takeover led by Butler. (Congressional Record, February 1934).

46 During the post–World War II hunt for political heresy in the New York educational system based on the McCarthy hearings, Morris Schappes was fired from his college position and jailed. He was charged with perjury after appearing before a legislative committee. (See *The American Inquisition* by Cedric Belfrage).

47 At the opening session of the 1937 Pittsburgh congress, the delegates cheered a message from Tom Mooney, a San Francisco labor union organizer. He had spent twenty years of a former life sentence in a California state prison for his alleged part in a bombing incident during a 1916 campaign to organize San Francisco trolley car workers. He was pardoned in 1939.

48 Among those who addressed the huge gathering at the Velodrome Buffalo on August 25, 1936, were Maurice Thorez, head of the Communist Party of France; Jacques Kaiser, a prominent journalist who was secretary-general of the French Radical Party; and Jean Ziromski, secretary of the Socialist Party's National Education Teachers Union (FEN).

49 Joseph Cadden, Edward Strong, Elizabeth Scott, Waldo McNutt, Gil Green, and myself.

50 Two months before the Washington meetings, League chairman Harry F. Ward asked Columbia University professor Walter Rautenstrauch to attend a meeting to consider how to draw more middle-class people into the peace and democracy movement. The professor also got involved with the League's finances. Despite its past success in organizing such large and impressive events as the annual congresses, the League was facing a critical financial situation. Rautenstrauch wrote to the members of the National Committee and the National Board explaining that the organization could not repay a $5,000 loan that was due. It had also been advised by the government that it was liable for social security and unemployment insurance benefit taxes since 1936. Rautenstrauch apprised the organization that both financial obligations might have to be met by individual members of the National Committee and

National Board. A follow-up letter to all branches reported that the national office staff had been receiving only half pay for three weeks.

51 A bill then in Congress was threatening to cut the Works Progress Administration (WPA) appropriations by $150 million. This would force the layoff of between 1,500,000 to 2,000,000 workers who had been on the WPA rolls for 18 months. It also required a loyalty oath of anyone seeking a new job. Despite a nationwide drive against the WPA cuts, the Senate approved by a 47 to 46 vote (January 27, 1939) to cut the funds. Many Democrats, including Senator Harry S. Truman, joined Republicans in reducing WPA funding.

52 Despite these adverse developments, the National Committee elected at the League congress in January, 1939, continued to reflect the organization's status and vitality. Its members included the prominent black educator Mary McLeod Bethune, founder of what became the Bethune-Cookman University; American Federation of Teachers' President, Jerome Davis: William M. Hinckley, former president of the American Youth Congress, who had become labor secretary of the League of Nations Association; David Lasser, president of the Workers Alliance, the leading organization of the unemployed; Dr. Reinhold Niebuhr of the Union Theological Seminary; chemistry professor Harold Urey (1934 winner of the Nobel Prize for the isolation of heavy hydrogen); Bishop Francis J. McConnell; and Molly Yard, executive secretary of the Far Eastern Student Service Fund. (Yard was a previous officer of the American Student Union who more than four decades later became leader of the National Organization of Women).

53 Several weeks later, some members of the ACLU's national board initiated a movement to oust Ward as ACLU chairman, claiming that his leadership role at the League conflicted with his role as ACLU chairman. Ward was eventually forced to resign as ACLU chairman.

54 When Dorothy McConnell died at age 90 in October 1989, the extensive New York Times obituary noted that she had been leader of the women's division of the Methodist Church and served on the national board of the YWCA. Unlike many of her associates at the American League Against War and Fascism, she was apparently never blacklisted by HUAC.

55 Prominent public figures quoted in the magazine *Friday* offered explanations for the despairing attitudes among youth. Poet Archibald MacLeish, Librarian of Congress, blamed the disaffection on antiwar writers. These included French novelist Henri Barbusse, a founder of the World Congress Against War and Fascism, and Americans John Dos Passos and Ernest Hemingway. A few novelists were thus blamed for the distrustful feelings of young Americans for whom poverty and fear of war were everyday realities. These young

people had worked for years in the antiwar movement and had marched, picketed, and struck by the millions against war and unemployment. What they rejected were the policies and morality of those who brought the country and the world to the brink of catastrophe.

56 Tom Wright was fired from his job as a reporter at the Schenectady, New York *Gazette* in the early 1930s for trying to organize a chapter of the American Newspaper Guild. He then offered to help a group of GE workers organize a union at the company's huge local plant by writing leaflets and helping distribute them at the plant gates. When the national union was formed in 1936, Wright accepted the invitation of Julius Emspak to come to New York City to direct its publicity efforts.

57 These articles included "UE Drive on Wage Discrimination Wins Cheers From Women Workers" (April 15, 1951) and "Why Women at Aerovax plant Chose UE—It's a Union that Fights for All Workers" (September 3, 1951). She wrote, "For 15 years this union has fought, more than any other union and against bitter company resistance, to eliminate lower rates for women." She further notes that a report issued by the Women's Bureau of the U.S. Department of Labor in September, 1951, acknowledges that in the electrical industry, equal pay for women was a result of UE's organizing activities. She also wrote a union pamphlet in 1952 entitled *UE Fights for Women Workers*, on the status of women in the electrical manufacturing industry and UE's efforts to eliminate discrimination.

58 At the invitation of General Douglas MacArthur, Tom Wright went to Japan at the end of World War II as part of a labor press delegation to examine labor relations in Japan.

59 Wylie Brown was operating well within the history of his corporation. Everyone familiar with labor history knows about the infamous "Bisbee Deportation." When copper miners went on strike in 1917 at the Phelps Dodge facility in Bisbee, Arizona, vigilantes under the direction of the sheriff rounded up the miners. They were thrown into railroad cattle cars several inches deep in manure, and abandoned 200 miles into the New Mexican desert. Fortunately, they were later rescued.

60 Twenty-three years later, in spring 1971, the local union reported to national union headquarters that conditions in the foundry had again been allowed to seriously deteriorate, and there was still insufficient ventilation on the pallet lines. In addition, workers had not received chest X-rays for two years because the company had dropped its program of annual X-rays instituted by union negotiations in 1948. As a result of a grievance filed by the union, the foundry agreed to update its X-ray equipment and reinstitute the program.

Acknowledgments

I am grateful to the numerous friends and colleagues who shared with me their experiences and encouraged me to write this book. I thank the following libraries for allowing me to conduct research in their archives: the New York Public Library's Rosika Schwimmer Peace Collection, the New York University's Tamiment Library and Robert F. Wagner Labor Archives, the Swarthmore College Peace Collection, and the Bancroft Library at the University of California, Berkeley. My children Betty and Richard Lerner gave me their unending support during the writing of the many drafts of this volume. I thank Anna Marie Taylor for offering to edit the manuscript and for her faith that it would one day surface in a published form. Finally, I wish to acknowledge and honor all the courageous people who have tirelessly dedicated themselves to building the peace and union movements in this country.

Editors' Acknowledgments: We wish to express our gratitude to all those who read the manuscript in its early stages and offered their comments and ideas. We thank Frank Emspak, emeritus professor at the School for Workers, University of Wisconsin, Madison, and managing editor and executive producer of Workers Independent News. Frank's father, Julius Emspak, was one of the early leaders of UE. Frank's insights also came directly from his own years of experience as a machinist and shop steward at locals of UE and IUE during the 1970s and 1980s. They also came out of his perspective as a teacher, labor historian and news editor. Peter Gilmore, former editor of UE News following James Lerner's retirement, who subsequently completed a PhD in American history, offered invaluable comments and editorial review. Based on their expertise in American history and their backgrounds within UE, Emspak and Gilmore were uniquely situated to review the Lerner manuscript. We cannot thank them enough for their assistance in making this book possible.

We thank UE for permission to use the union logo that appears at the beginning of Part Three. Grateful acknowledgment is made to Robin Ward Savage for permission to use the Lynd Ward woodcut. We would like to thank Julie Greene and Mary Kay Vaughan for their good counsel and insights into the meaning of this book. We were buoyed throughout this endeavor by the constant support we received from David Asarnow, Thea Lerner Daniels and David Daniels, Linda Lustig, Avis Taylor and Jim Thomas, and Jannie Taylor. We are also indebted to Sarah Chavez and Marge Renfroe for their meticulous proofreading, questions and advice.

Index

15308429R00131

Made in the USA
Charleston, SC
28 October 2012